HOW TO TOILET TRAIN YOUR CAT

& 61 OTHER ILL-CONCEIVED PROJECTS

MAR 16

"It takes half your life before you discover life is a do-it-yourself project."

—Napoleon Hill

"You tried your best and you failed miserably. The lesson is never try."

—Homer Simpson

UNCLE JOHN'S
HOW TO TOILET TRAIN YOUR CAT

Copyright © 2015 by Portable Press.

Portable Press is an imprint of the Printers Row Publishing Group
A Division of Readerlink Distribution Services, LLC

"Bathroom Reader," "Portable Press," and "Bathroom Readers' Institute"
are registered trademarks of Readerlink Distribution Services, LLC. All
rights reserved

For information, write: The Bathroom Readers' Institute,
P.O. Box 1117, Ashland, OR 97520
www.bathroomreader.com

Cover design by Andy Taray (ohioboy.com)
Illustrations by Shea Strauss (sheastrauss.com)
Interior design by Lidija Tomas

Library of Congress Cataloging-in-Publication Data

Uncle John's how to toilet train your cat.
    pages cm
  ISBN 978-1-62686-360-6 (hardcover)
1. American wit and humor. 2. Curiosities and wonders. I. Bathroom
Readers' Institute (Ashland, Or.) II. Title: How to toilet train your cat.
  PN6165.U53668 2015
  081--dc23
                    2014036910

Printed in the United States of America
First Printing: June 2015
19 18 17 16 15   1 2 3 4 5

THANK YOU!

The Bathroom Readers' Institute sincerely thanks the people whose advice and assistance made this book possible.

Gordon Javna	Dan Mansfield
Brian Boone	Kim Griswell
Lidija Tomas	Jay Newman
Andy Taray	Dave Blees
Christy Taray	Aaron Guzman
Shea Strauss	Blake Mitchum
Trina Janssen	Rusty von Dyl
Brandon Hartley	J. Carroll
Jack Feerick	David Hoye
Pablo Goldstein	Jennifer and Mana
Ben Godar	Melinda Allman
Megan Todd	Peter Norton
Julie McLaughlin	Lilian Nordland

CONTENTS

DO NOT TRY THIS AT HOME!

Greetings, risk-takers. My name is Dwayne O. Flushman, chief counsel for Uncle John, the Bathroom Readers' Institute, and senior partner in the lawfirm of Plummer, Plummer & Piper.

My client set out to personally test all 63 projects in this book, but succumbed to radiation sickness while trying to build an X-ray machine. That was the first one he tried; he didn't get to the rest. Let my legal proclamations (and Uncle John's personal misfortune) dissuade you from actually attempting to replicate any of the fascinating plans you encounter in *How to Toilet Train Your Cat*.

The Bathroom Readers' Institute publishes trivia books, and humor books. The book in your hands is both of those things; *it is not a manual of any kind.*

In this book you'll read about how to do or make all kinds of things. Here are some of those things you'll learn how to do...but *absolutely must not do*:

• How to perform open heart surgery, how to give yourself hair plugs, and how to remove your own appendix

- How to make cigarettes, batteries, film, and replications of priceless artworks
- How to craft candles, glue, and gelatin...the old-fashioned ways
- How to build a roller coaster, a swimming pool, or a sports car...in your backyard
- How to toilet train your cat

Actually...that last one is fine. But *only* that one.

The vast majority of the these do-it-yourself capers can and will endanger your life, your property, the life and property of others, or your spotless criminal record. We realize that many of the required steps and materials are undoable and unattainble...but that's the point. This is a book that shows you how things are made, in what we think is a fun way.

Nevertheless, we are not legally responsible if you are dumb enough to actually attempt these tasks, which, frankly, are impossible to try by a person who isn't infinitely wealthy, infinitely insane, or both.

Sincerely,

**The Bathroom Readers' Institute,
and its legal advisors**

HOW TO BUILD AN X-RAY MACHINE

As seen in the book
How to Build an X-Ray Machine.

WHAT YOU'LL NEED

- X-ray tube
- High-voltage power supply
- Electrical tape
- Five alligator clips
- At least eight feet of 12-gauge AWG wire
- Six-inch tabletop fan
- Insulating rubber (or Styrofoam)
- Velcro strips
- Lead sheets
- Geiger counter
- Lead apron
- Wooden boards

THE X-FACTOR

Except when you're turning the power supply on or off, don't stand any closer than eight inches to the power supply, wires, alligator clips, terminals—well, the entire X-ray machine in general. Unplug it and wait a minute before moving or handling anything. That much electricity—30,000 volts—can and will jump several inches. You don't want to electrocute or radiate yourself to death because of some dumb project in a dumb book.

DO IT YOURSELF!

1. Put on your lead apron.

2. Connect the power supply to the X-ray tube with the 12-gauge wire. Keep everything in place with some of the alligator clips. (Don't plug in or turn anything on...yet.)

3. Double-check to make sure that you connected the X-ray tube correctly, in terms of polarization, so that power flows. This means that the positive terminal on the power supply should be connected to the tip of the tube, and the negative end of the supply to the base pins of the X-ray tube.

4. Once you've confirmed that everything is properly connected, wrap the alligator clips in electrical tape, and then wrap the X-ray tube in electrical tape. This is a safety measure, but it also ensures that the clips will stay in place and do their job (which is also a safety measure).

5. Mount and orient the power supply and X-ray tube onto wooden boards. This will make your X-ray device portable—so you can take it to a friend's house or something—but it's also a good idea to have your radiation-generating machine be an easily contained one.

6. Glue Velcro to the machinery and the wood, and stick the Velcro pieces to each other to keep the equipment in place. Feed wires through the board slats as necessary.

7. Set up the radiation shielding material around the X-ray tube. This is a *vital* safety precaution. Lead is the easiest option, because it's commonly sold in 0.4-inch-thick sheets. To ensure you have a safely operating X-ray machine, place three sheets' worth of the lead around the X-ray tube to make for a 1.2-inch-thick safety shield. Make sure to place it between the tube and the power supply—this prevents anyone from being exposed to radiation when reaching to turn the machine on or off.

8. Keep a small opening in the shielding somewhere for ventilation and cooling. Why? This will prevent overheating and/or radioactive fires, both of which are very bad.

9. Where exactly you place the shielding depends on how you'll use the X-ray machine. If you want to irradiate objects (or living things) at close range, shield the entire tube except for the ventilation hole. If you're more interested in using the machine to take X-ray images, leave an opening in the side of the top so a small but controlled stream of X-rays can escape to make those images possible. Just make sure not to point that hole toward where you might stand or walk by while the machine is running.

10. If you're on the second story or higher of a multiple-story building, place shielding below the X-ray machine. Also, if there are people on the floors above you, make a tent of lead-sheet shielding above the machine, too.

11. Now that the shielding is in place, check your wires again. High-voltage wires improperly attached can and will start fires, so make sure that there aren't any exposed ends, and that they aren't touching or about to touch any other part of the machine.

12. Insulate the lead from the wires by wrapping the wires in Styrofoam or rubber.

13. Place the fan in the shielding area. This circulates air around the tube and out through the ventilation opening. (Otherwise, the heat generated by the machine ironically interferes with X-ray imaging.)

14. Place the machine in a corner of a room with thick walls. Tell others not to bother you for a while, so as to limit their exposure to radiation on the off chance that you didn't assemble your X-ray machine correctly. This quarantine order includes pets.

15. Test to make sure that it works, and that it's safe. With the machine unplugged, turn

on the Geiger counter to get a baseline or "background radiation" level.

16. Stand behind the X-ray machine, away from the ventilation hole. Turn on the fan, plug in the power supply, crank up the X-ray machine to 30,000 volts. Your machine, if all went well, is on and shooting off all kinds of X-rays.

17. Standing behind the shielding, take a reading with the Geiger counter. If the reading from outside the machine is above 300 uRem per hour, immediately turn off the machine, unplug it, and add another layer or two of lead sheeting. (In fact, you might just want to do that anyway.)

NOW THIS IS SHOCKING

If you were to make this with supplies purchased through places like United Nuclear, Nuclead, and Radio Shack, you'll end up spending about $575. Now, say you fracture your hip, go to a U.S. hospital, and have a couple of X-rays taken. Estimated cost (before insurance): about $900.

HOW TO PERFORM OPEN HEART SURGERY

Heart surgery can cost hundreds of thousands of dollars even after health insurance kicks in. Don't blow your lifetime nachos budget on some doctor and hospital—do it yourself. You've got this.

WHAT YOU'LL NEED

- A patient
- Sterile operating room
- Cardiopulmonary bypass (heart-lung) machine
- Scalpel
- Bone saw
- Surgical wire
- Various clamps and sponges
- Silk sutures
- Anesthesia
- Anticoagulant drugs
- Cardiology textbooks
- Pacemaker (optional)
- New heart (optional)

HAVE A HEART

The cardiopulmonary bypass machine also cools the blood, inducing a state of hypothermia that helps to protect the patient from brain damage. A state-of-the-art model will cost you about $100,000, but used ones occasionally turn up on eBay. Really.

DO IT YOURSELF!

1. Are you *really* going to do this yourself? At least take a couple of anatomy and physiology classes to prepare, or go all the way and graduate from medical school. At the very least, read a couple of cardiology textbooks.

2. Sterilize your tools, sterilize your operating room, and sterilize the patient.

WIDE OPEN

As you undoubtedly learned at the medical school you attended between steps, "open heart surgery" is a technique, rather than one specific operation.

3. Prepare the patient for surgery. Anesthetize him with real anesthesia—a few slugs of bourbon isn't going to cut it. It's in everyone's best interest if the patient is asleep.

4. Take your scalpel and expose the left breastbone by making an incision straight down the center of the chest, about nine inches long.

5. Saw through the bone to access the heart. It's the pulsating red thing on the left. No, the *patient's* left. *Your* right.

6. Hook up the heart-lung machine by inserting cannulas into the *vena cava* (to withdraw blood from the body) and the ascending aorta (to put it back in). Now you're ready to replace a clogged artery, install a pacemaker, or even perform a full heart transplant.

7. Reverse the heart-lung machine, restoring the flow of blood to the heart.

8. Check your work for leaks; if everything looks sound, it's time to close up. Wire the breastbone shut, and then close the incision with regular silk sutures.

9. When the patient wakes up—*if* the patient wakes up—present your bill.

HOW TO MAKE PENCILS

Pencils are cheap, and you might use one every day.
That doesn't mean they're easy to make.

WHAT YOU'LL NEED

- Graphite
- Fine clay
- Extruder
- Kiln
- Cedar planks
- Wood stain
- Wax
- Wood grinder
- Wood planer
- Wood glue
- Nontoxic yellow paint
- Aluminum
- Synthetic rubber powder
- Pink dye
- Vegetable oil
- Pumice
- Sulfur
- Pencil sharpener

GREEK TO YOU

How much lead is in a pencil lead? None. The writing material is made of graphite, a naturally occurring material very similar to lead. The name comes from *graphein*, a Greek word that means "to write."

DO IT YOURSELF!

1. Ground the graphite and mix with fine clay. The higher the ratio of clay to graphite, the harder and darker the lead.

2. Use an extruder to shape the mixture into a long, thin rod. Bake the graphite-clay mixture in a kiln set to 2,200°F until it hardens.

3. Let cool, and then coat the rod with wax. This will make for smoother writing.

4. Cut the cedar plank down to a rectangular slat that's 7.25 inches long, 2.75 inches wide, and a quarter of an inch thick. This method should yield six uniform pencils.

5. Use some wood stain to paint the cedar plank, let dry, and then treat it with wax. This prevents warping during construction. After the wax dries, plane each side of the plank to smooth out the outer surfaces.

6. Cut the wood in half, so you end up with two 8-inch-thick slats.

7. Measure the width of the graphite rods you've already made. Cut six grooves, lengthwise, into each of the two slats.

8. Cut the long graphite rods into six smaller rods. Lay each rod down in the groove on one of the cedar planks.

9. Fit the other slat on top, and use wood glue to affix the two slats together.

> **WRITE ON!**
>
> • About 1.6 million pencils are manufactured…every hour.
>
> • Number 1 or number 2? The higher the number on a pencil, the darker the writing.

10. Paint with yellow nontoxic paint. Why nontoxic? So you can chew on them when you're thinking, of course.

11. But what good is a pencil without an eraser? (If you don't ever make mistakes, you might as well use a pen, and there isn't an article in this book on how to make pens.) So, start by installing on your pencils some ferrules— those are the little metal doodads that hold the eraser on a pencil. Cut six ¼-inch pieces of thin aluminum and roll them into six metal loops. Glue one roll to each of the pencils.

12. Mix synthetic rubber powder with pink dye, vegetable oil, pumice, and sulfur. Heat the mixture to 280°F. The heat will make the sulfur vulcanize, rendering the rubber more stable and pliable.

13. Force the soft solid rubber through an extruder to form a long cylinder.

14. Cut the rubber into ½-inch plugs.

15. Insert one plug into each pencil's ferrule and use pliers to gently clamp the metal shut over the rubber.

16. Sharpen your pencil and go ace that standardized test, or draw a nice picture of Grandma.

HOW TO WEAR A BEARD OF BEES

*All the hipsters these days have beards, but
here's a way to make yours really stand out.
(Hint: It's bees.)*

WHAT YOU'LL NEED

- Bees. At least a few hundred, or as many as a thousand.
- A queen bee, preferably a young one
- Beehive box
- Bee-feeding tray
- Plenty of sugar syrup
- Bee smoker
- Nasonov, a bee pheromone
- Plastic vial
- Necklace chain

BEE SHARP!

- Organized beekeeping dates to 2500 BC, but a Ukrainian beekeeper named Petro Prokopovych invented bee bearding in 1850 to show off how well he got along with his bees.

- The Clovermead Bee Beard Competition takes place every summer at a farm in Quebec. Past participants have danced and even hula-hooped with their faces covered in bees.

DO IT YOURSELF!

1. Gather your supplies—farm-and-feed stores generally carry beekeeping stuff. Head to an open area a safe distance from densely populated spaces. A shopping mall, for example, is not an appropriate place to experiment with bee bearding.

2. Get your bees in the "right mood." How do you calm down a bunch of bees? Feed them all the sugar syrup they can get their mandibles on. Fill the feeding tray with the stuff and place it in their box a full two days beforehand. Keep the syrup flowing.

3. Once 48 hours have come and gone, your bees should be so overfed and mellow that they can't fly off in search of nectar, let alone sting you. Remove the lid from their box, find the queen, and place her in the plastic vial.

4. Despite their lethargy, the bees will instinctively "swarm" and follow their queen, especially if it's a young queen. The younger the queen, the stronger the pheromones she

excretes and the more likely she is to have a devoted hive that will buzz after her wherever she goes. Attach the vial to the necklace, place it around your neck, and stand beside the box.

5. If your bees are still sugar drunk and not interested in seeing what their queen is up to, spray some Nasonov into the box to give them a little boost. This will help them orient themselves and fly over to the queen.

6. Within a few minutes, more and more bees will start crawling all over your neck and face, trying to get to the queen.

7. Try to stay as calm as possible. If you start running around and waving your arms, for example, this could cause the bees to freak out and start stinging you.

8. What happens next is up to you. You could head over to a coffeehouse (and cause everyone to panic) or a day care center (and cause everyone to panic) or a beekeepers' convention (where people will probably just

roll their eyes and go back to what they were doing). The bees will hang out on your face as long as their queen is in that vial. However, if her pheromones are powerful enough, she may attract bees from other hives in the area—ones that aren't full of syrup and wouldn't mind stinging you.

9. When you've somehow grown bored with thousands of insects crawling around on your body, remove the vial, take out the queen, and gently place her back in the box.

10. As crazy as it might sound, jump up in the air to remove the bees. It really works—jostled off your face when your feet hit the ground, the bees will calmly head back to their box.

11. At this point, a "professional" bee bearder would employ an assistant to "smoke" the bees to encourage all of them to head into the box. If you're doing this on your own, smoke them yourself. The bees don't really like this very much; prepare to get stung up to a dozen times.

12. Once all the bees are off you, put the lid back on the box, check your clothing for any stragglers, and congratulate yourself on not getting stung to death.

HOW TO MAKE HIGH-FRUCTOSE CORN SYRUP

*More sugar, honey? Here's a corny
way to make the sweetest thing.*

WHAT YOU'LL NEED

- About 10 cups of corn, specifically a variety called "Yellow Dent #2"
- Food mill
- Sulfuric acid
- Bacterial enzymes:
  - Alpha-amylase
  - Glucose-amylase
  - Xylose
- Glucose isomerase, a genetically engineered chemical compound
- Eyedropper
- Rubber gloves
- Slow cooker
- Cheesecloth (for hard cheeses)
- Wooden spoons
- Candy thermometer
- Glass jar
- Stockpots
- Water
- Food-grade diatomaceous earth

DO IT YOURSELF!

1. Ground the corn until it's a chunky powder.

2. Fill a stockpot with 8 cups of water. Put on the rubber gloves and add in one drop of sulfuric acid. (At a ratio of 200 parts per million, it's *fairly* safe for human consumption.)

3. Cover the pot, and boil the water/acid mixture until it reaches a steady temperature between 140° and 160°F.

THE SWEET LIFE

HFCS was first developed in the mid-1970s. Agribusiness conglomerates such as Archer Daniels Midland were dealt a huge financial blow with the rise of the soybean industry, which had introduced cheap, high-quality, shelf-stable, soy-derived margarine. Seeking a new, lucrative market, scientists at several corn processors worked together to come up with HFCS, basically a modern adaptation of corn syrup, a corn-based sweetener created in the 1920s. The difference is that high-fructose corn syrup, as the name implies, has high amounts of fructose, and the way it's made allows for very tight control of the proportion of ingredients.

4. Pour in the ground corn and let it sit until the temperature returns to 140°F.

5. Turn on the slow cooker and pour in the corn slurry. Let it sit for 24 hours, simmering at 140°F.

6. The next day, add a teaspoon of the alpha-amylase. Stir with a wooden spoon.

7. Turn off the slow cooker. Add one teaspoon of glucose-amylase and let the enzyme soak into the corn as it cools for about 20 minutes, or until the mixture is at room temperature.

HOW SWEET IT IS

• Basically, HFCS is enzyme-treated cornstarch. The enzymes break down complex corn sugar molecules into simpler ones, a process that isolates the glucose and then converts it to a mixture that is made up of exactly 55% fructose.

• It brings in $3 billion a year for the four companies that make it.

8. Place the cheesecloth over another large stockpot. Pour in the cooled corn mixture—if it looks like regurgitated creamed corn, you're doing it right. Sprinkle onto the corn one teaspoon of xylose powder.

9. Put on some more rubber gloves and strain the liquid from the corn slurry while also gently incorporating the xylose.

10. Once you've extracted every possible bit of moisture from the corn, throw the weird yellow ball of corn powder away. The liquid strained through the cheesecloth is what you're after.

11. Take that brownish-yellowish liquid and pour it back into the slow cooker. Add two eyedroppers full of glucose isomerase. Heat until the liquid boils.

12. While it's boiling, add a teaspoon of glycose amylase.

13. Keep the liquid boiling for one minute. Then, turn the slow cooker down to low and let it simmer for 15 minutes.

14. Remove the syrup from the heat and pour it into a clean jar.

15. You've now made a usable, *incredibly* sweet sugar substitute...one that's brownish-yellow and tastes like corn. Before the concoction begins to separate, filter it through diatomaceous earth. That will remove the color and corniness.

16. Return the syrup to a clean stockpot and boil to release impurities and to reduce it to a thicker, clearer syrup.

17. Use the syrup to sweeten soda, bread, waffles, candy bars, baking mixes, ketchup, tomato sauce, cough syrup, crackers, juice, soup...

THE WHITE STUFF

Despite the lengthy manufacturing process and the chemicals involved, HFCS is cheaper for food production than sugar. There's far more corn grown in the continental U.S. than sugar (sugar is imported from Hawaii and the Caribbean), and corn production is even subsidized by the government.

HOW TO MAKE WHITE SUGAR

Did you know that "bone char" is used to refine cane sugar from its raw, brown, chunky origins into little white granules you put in your coffee?

DO IT YOURSELF!

1. Heat some cow bones at a high temperature until they're black and have a charcoal-like consistency. No longer bones, they've broken down into their core elements of carbon and calcium phosphate.

2. Place the char in a filter and pass liquid cane sugar through it. The bone char will naturally attract the impurities that would otherwise make sugar not white.

3. Allow the liquid sugar to crystallize, and it will become an angelic white.

HOW TO MAKE A SHRUNKEN HEAD

No, we're not talking about psychiatry.

WHAT YOU'LL NEED

- A head, no longer in use
- Needle
- Thread
- A sharp knife
- A pot
- Jungle herbs
- Large stones
- Slightly smaller stones
- Pebbles
- Ashes
- Berry juice
- Scissors

GETTING AHEAD

We're referring to the process of collecting and preserving the heads of vanquished enemies, as set forth by the Jivaro tribe, who used to do this in the jungles of Ecuador and Peru. As Western explorers came in increasing contact with Jivaro in the late 19th century, shrunken heads became a popular souvenir. Traders would barter guns, ammo, and other useful items for shrunken heads.

DO IT YOURSELF!

1. Peel the skin and hair away from the skull. Discard the skull.

2. Sew the eye and mouth openings closed. This is done to trap the soul inside—you don't want the person's ghost to come back and haunt you!

3. Turn the fleshy face that remains inside out. Scrape the fat away with a sharp knife.

4. Add some jungle herbs to a pot of water and bring to a boil.

5. Throw in the head and let it simmer for two hours.

6. Remove the head from the water, and fill it with hot stones. Roll the head on a flat surface constantly to prevent the hot stones from scorching the head.

7. The head will slowly start to shrink. As it does so, remove the hot stones every

15 minutes or so and replace them with progressively smaller hot stones. At each rock replacement break, mold the facial features so the head keeps its shape and distinctive facialness.

8. Hang over a fire to dry.

9. Polish it with ashes, and then moisturize with berry juice. This will prevent cracking.

10. Once it's cool and dry, sew the neck hole closed.

11. Trim the hair to the style of your choice.

CHILD'S PLAY

The Jivaro were constantly at war with neighboring tribes, and collected the heads of their fallen enemies as war trophies. Paraded around during celebrations, they were then discarded… or given to Jivaro children as toys.

HOW TO CONSTRUCT AN ATOMIC BOMB

*So you're a death-crazed maniac and you're tired of
the more pedestrian methods of mass destruction.
You're ready to go nuclear! But where to start?*

WHAT YOU'LL NEED

- About 14 pounds of plutonium-239 (retail price: $24 million)
- A neutron initiator, such as a pellet of polonium the size of a marble
- Two crucibles
- Brackets
- 5 grams of gold
- 5 grams of nickel
- Two concentric aluminum spheres
- Conventional explosive, such as C4
- 32 explosive lens units
- An exploding bridgewire detonator
- Lead-lined gloves
- Facemask
- Lead apron
- HAZMAT suit
- Lead-lined box
- Cylinder of hydrogen isotope, such as deuterium or tritium

DO IT YOURSELF!

1. Mill and form your plutonium into two bowl shapes, leaving a hollow in the middle of each. When locked together, they should form a sphere about the size of a grapefruit. The plutonium is fairly stable at this stage, so there's no danger of explosion. However, touching or inhaling the stuff can still mess you up, so wear gloves, a facemask, and a lead apron.

2. Insert brackets into the hollows to hold the polonium pellet; *do not* assemble the sphere yet.

3. Move to a different, safe, and—most important—remote location (like an atoll in the Pacific), and get into full protective gear to begin work on the neutron initiator. The polonium is not only super-toxic on its own, but its very presence can trigger an explosive reaction in the plutonium.

4. Melt the gold and the nickel in separate crucibles. Dunk the polonium into the nickel

to coat; let cool, then repeat with the gold. This is your neutron initiator; set it aside (preferably in a lead-lined box) until ready to use.

5. Install the C4 charges in the bomb's outer shell, using the explosive lens units to direct the full force of the blast inward. Your aim is to create an implosion in the core, so precision is quite important. Also, make sure to use enough C4 to line the interior of this, the outermost sphere.

6. Install the exploding bridgewire detonator. Set it so that all the charges will go off simultaneously.

7. When you're ready to use your atomic bomb, insert the neutron initiator into the brackets in the hollow of the plutonium sphere, and carefully fit the sphere together. Insert this core into the shell lined with conventional explosives, and get yourself a safe distance away—say, several hundred miles.

THE NON-NUCLEAR OPTION

If a full-on atom bomb is out of your budget, a dirty bomb, also known as a radiological dispersal device (RDD), is your best option. RDDs use TNT, C4, or some concoction of fertilizer to scatter radioactive debris over a wide area. The nuclear material in an RDD does not cause the explosion—it's just the payload, like the roofing nails in a pipe bomb—so it doesn't have to be a weapons-grade isotope. Even materials used in hospitals and power plants could potentially be repurposed for a dirty bomb. The odds of anyone actually getting sick or dying from radiation are slim. But if your aim is simply to cause panic, this one's hard to beat.

8. When the C4 charges are triggered, the resulting implosion compresses the plutonium and destroys the protective coating of the neutron initiator. The polonium starts shooting out alpha particles, breaking the electromagnetic bonds in some of the atoms of the plutonium, which in turn sets off a chain reaction. The atoms fly apart, releasing massive concussive force and intense heat. This is nuclear fission (what they used to call "splitting the atom") and it can produce a blast equivalent to thousands of tons of TNT—enough to mess

Handmade
with *love!*

up the countryside for miles around with a triple whammy of shockwave, fire, and lethal radiation.

9. For an even bigger boom, use the cylinder of hydrogen isotope to create a two-stage thermonuclear device. Install your completed spherical fission bomb atop the cylinder, like a dot atop a lowercase letter "i," and detonate as usual. The heat and X-rays of the fission reaction compress the hydrogen isotope, triggering a fusion reaction with a concussive force equivalent to 10.5 million tons of dynamite.

10. Promise to use your power only for good. (Optional)

HOW TO DISMANTLE AN ATOMIC BOMB

First, the good news: An atomic fission reaction is triggered by conventional explosives, so defusing an atomic bomb is a pretty much the same as defusing a conventional bomb. But here's the weird thing: You can actually prevent the atomic reaction even if the conventional charges go off.

To trigger a fission reaction, the full force of the chemical explosion must be symmetrically focused inward toward the plutonium core. The bomb must remain sealed, and the baffles that direct the kinetic force must be properly aligned. If any of that force is dispersed outward, the core won't blow.

So before you try cutting any wires, halting an electronic timer, start prying off pieces of the bomb casing, or just start poking holes in the thing. The force of the explosion (if it occurs) will be vented away from the core; without the full force, the core will not compress, the chain reaction will not start, and you won't have to start looking for a new city to live in.

DO YOUR OWN LIPOSUCTION AND SAVE!

Who among us isn't carrying a little extra fat we'd like to get rid of? You could try diet and exercise, but who has the time?

WHAT YOU'LL NEED

- Local anesthetic, such as lidocaine, laced with a mild sedative to reduce anxiety but not put you to sleep
- Syringe

- Thin surgical tube, or cannula
- Scalpel
- Saline solution
- Medical-grade suction pump, or a modified high-powered handheld vacuum, like a Dyson model
- Compression garment, such as Spanx
- Disinfectant
- Medical twine
- Needle

THIS SUCKS

Once you add up the price of the operation itself, along with anesthesia and all the other little costs, even a small procedure can cost upward of $10,000.

DO IT YOURSELF!

1. Liposuction, while a mild and elective medical procedure, is a medical procedure nonetheless. Consider employing the use of a "surgical buddy." Since you will be operating on yourself and may become groggy from the anesthetic, it's a good idea to have a friend there to drive you to the hospital if things go awry.

2. Apply the local anesthetic and thoroughly disinfect your workspace, your abdomen, and all your tools.

3. Make a small incision in your stomach and insert a small metal tube (cannula) into your chubby area. Be sure to dig and get down to the *deeper* layers of subcutaneous fat, where you are less likely to damage your skin.

4. Move the cannula back and forth vigorously to break up those pesky fat cells. You may want to pump a saline solution (along with additional lidocaine) through the cannula during this process to prevent skin dents, minimize blood loss, and avoid the unpleasant and painful

burning of fat from all that friction.

TRIMMING THE FAT

What do doctors do with the fat after they remove it? It's burned in an industrial incinerator and then sent as medical waste to landfills. (Or you could make a candle out of it. Turn to page 77.)

5. Here's where the "suction" in "liposuction" comes from. Once you've broken up the fat cells, you need to suck them out with the suction pump or vacuum. Don't be shy and don't be gentle—that fat doesn't want to go any-where, and you've come this far. Get all of it!

6. Sew up the wound, and compress it. You've removed a layer of living tissue from inside your body, and now your body has to heal. Wrap the area or wear some kind of compression garment, like Spanx, to speed the healing process and reduce internal bleeding. Sure, you're probably performing liposuction on yourself so you won't have to wear those control garments anymore. But they can come in very handy one last time, as they compress your wound...and keep you from bleeding to death.

HOW TO FORGE A MASTERPIECE

In 2012, Paul Cézanne's The Card Players *sold for $250 million. Painted in the 19th century, the piece features two guys playing cards. That's it. No Picasso curves or Van Gogh landscapes. It's the sort of thing that, with practice, someone could replicate. Someone like you!*

WHAT YOU'LL NEED

- Art stuff, like canvases, paintbrushes, a sponge brush, and frames
- Coarse sandpaper
- Fine-grit sandpaper
- Varnish
- Raw umber craft paint
- Burnt umber paint
- Egg yolks
- Mortar and pestle
- Various minerals, including hematite
- Paint that will look appropriate to the era in which the final product was said to have been created
- A skilled and shady art dealer
- An art studio far away from prying eyes

DO IT YOURSELF!

1. Choose an art movement. Do you want to become skilled at cubism like Georges Braque and Pablo Picasso? Or do you think you'd be better at impressionism or romanticism? Once you've got a movement picked out, practice, practice, and practice some more. Take some art classes to further hone the basic painting techniques that helped history's greatest artists make their masterpieces.

2. Select the masterpiece that you want to forge. Don't choose the *Mona Lisa*, for example, because everybody knows that it's hanging in the Louvre in Paris. Instead, choose a lesser-known work, or a masterpiece that was lost or stolen long ago. For example, you could go with Raphael's *Portrait of a Young Man*. It was looted by the Nazis and is still missing.

COPYCAT!

Art forgery is nothing new. Historians theorize that copycats were faking famous works as early as the 1st century AD.

Art experts think it could sell for as much as $100 million of it's ever recovered (or if an expert forgery turns up).

3. If you can't find 500-year-old Italian paint, you'll have to improvise your own. There weren't a lot of paint stores during the Renaissance, so artists back then improvised too, often making their own supplies. Do what they did, and mix egg yolks with various minerals and pigments to get the colors needed. Let's stick with red for now. Grab some hematite, toss it in a mortar, grind it down, throw in a little bit of egg yolk, and add some water until you get the hue you need.

4. Once you've got the right red, move on to black, purple, yellow, and whatever other colors you might need. Because this paint has egg yolk in it, it won't keep well for longer than a few hours. Only mix up what you need.

5. Start painting. Don't get discouraged if it takes you a dozen or even hundreds of times to re-create the masterpiece. Keep going until

you've got a copy that would fool the average person.

6. Using more of your not-really-old old paint, re-create the masterpiece on the canvas and, once the paint is dry, age it appropriately. If you've selected *Portrait of a Young Man*, for example, you'll need to make sure that it looks like it was painted back in the early 16th century. The best way to do this is to falsely age the canvas. Sand down the painting with coarse sandpaper. Then go over it again

• To spite imitators in the 1500s, German artist Albrecht Dürer added the words "be cursed, plunderers and imitators of the work and talent of others" to one of his paintings.

• Early in his career, Michelangelo tried to make some easy money forging art. He sculpted a cupid and aged it so that it looked centuries old. Unfortunately, the buyer didn't fall for the ruse and demanded his money back.

with a fine-grit sandpaper until you've got a smooth finish. Carefully wipe away any remaining dust or debris.

7. With the sponge brush, apply a few coats of varnish. Allow it to dry.

8. Coat the edges of the canvas in raw umber craft paint—it replicates the slight browning that would otherwise come with time. Allow time to dry.

9. Take the burnt umber paint and, with a thin brush, paint on some fake cracks in the

canvas. Add a few to the perimeter and make them look like little tree branches.

10. Fake some *craquelure*. These are the dense cracks common on old paintings. Let it dry.

11. Grab a sponge brush, add two more coats of varnish, and—BOOM—you should have a painting that will make the uninitiated art novice think they're looking at something that's centuries old.

12. Take your painting to a skilled but totally corrupt art dealer who's willing to participate in this crazy scheme. Have the dealer inspect your painting and, if he or she is also convinced that it will fool the experts, move on to the next step.

13. Allow the dealer to find a sucker willing to spend millions of dollars on your obviously fake masterpiece. Once the deal is made, cash the check as quickly as you can, give your dealer a cut of the profits, and flee to an undisclosed location. If you selected

a high-profile painting like Raphael's missing masterpiece, it's going to inevitably encounter lots of scrutiny from art experts, the media, etc. By the time all of that unfolds, you'll want to be blowing your millions on piña coladas and speedboats someplace that's both tropical and laid back when it comes to extradition laws. If you're caught by the authorities, you could face many years in prison and severe financial penalties for your little art project.

THE LOST ART OF LOST ART

• Picasso's cubist masterpiece *Le pigeon aux petits pois*, reportedly worth at least $28 million, has been missing since 2010. A thief absconded with it, but then panicked and threw it in a trash can. The trash was then emptied, the trash hauled away, and the painting was never seen again. (Perhaps you could "find" *Le pigeon!*)

• If you're not so hot at cubism, you could re-create Jan van Eyck's *The Just Judges*. This 15th-century painting was stolen form a museum in Ghent, Belgium, in 1934. Later that year, suspected thief Arsène Goedertier made a deathbed confession, admitting to lifting the piece…but adding that he'd take the location of *The Just Judges* to his grave. Which is exactly what he did.

HOW TO MAKE PAINT

It stays on the walls for years.
What even is that stuff?

WHAT YOU'LL NEED

- Low-viscosity liquid solvent
- Synthetic pigments
- Iron oxide (rust)
- Blood
- Charcoal
- Fruit juice
- Linseed oil
- High-speed mixer
- Paint additives
- Vats

COLOR YOUR WORLD

• Plato was the first person to record the discovery that mixing two colors can make a third.

• Purple became associated with royalty during classical antiquity because they were the only people rich enough to afford the hard-to-make pigment.

• Humanity's oldest paintings have been found in caves in France and Spain. Images of animals and hands, they're as much as 40,000 years old. (What did they use for paint? Blood, charcoal, and clay.)

DO IT YOURSELF!

1. First you'll need to acquire a pigment, which will serve as your paint's color. Everything from synthetic pigments made in labs to iron oxide scraped off your rusty gardening tools will work. The latter is slightly more cost-effective.

2. Next you'll need a low-viscosity liquid solvent like alcohol or acetone for dilution purposes. This helps you to apply the paint—otherwise you'll basically be trying to paint with dried paint.

3. The third thing you need is a resin, usually linseed oil, to help the paint dry once you apply it—a very important ingredient, unless you want your house, room, or masterpiece to have that "permanent wet" look.

4. Last, you'll need additives, which will vary depending on what kind of paint you're trying to make. Paint properties you should consider include how fast it dries, mold resistance, and water resistance.

5. Once you have all your ingredients, you'll need to break down the pigment, which tends to clump together. Slowly add your pigment to a high-speed mixer and get it fine and dispersed.

GET THE LEAD OUT

Poisonous lead-based paint was first formulated as early as the 4th century BC in ancient Greece, and texts from the era warn that painters who worked with lead paint often suffered from epilepsy and paralysis. Germany established laws in 1886 banning women and children from working in lead paint factories, and in 1904 the Sherwin-Williams paint company began phasing lead out of its products. Lead paint wasn't banned in the U.S. until 1978.

6. As you gradually add pigment, slowly add in a little bit of your solvent and resin to prevent it from clumping together. The resulting product is called the mill-base.

7. In a separate vat, mix together the solvent, resin, and additives until they're combined to create the let-down.

8. While stirring the let-down, pour your mill-base into this vat and let it all blend together. You're now ready to paint!

HOW TO MAKE SAUSAGE

We've all heard the old saying, "You don't want to know how the sausage is made." It's a metaphorical statement, but here is how sausage really is made.

WHAT YOU'LL NEED

- Remnants of an animal carcass (literally anything will work)
- Intestines or other organs (often from a pig or cow, but again, whatever works)
- Meat grinder (or industrial-grade meat recovery equipment)
- Sharp knife
- Sieve
- Spices

LOW CULTURE

Probiotic starter cultures are strains of bacteria required to make many different kinds of sausage. In 2014, a team of food scientists in Spain discovered that three strains of bacteria contained those cultures, and that those bacteria are abundant in a very familiar, if very disgusting place: baby poop. The report was published in *Food Microbiology*, but so far Hormel, Oscar Mayer, and other commercial sausage makers have yet to jump on this.

DO IT YOURSELF!

1. You can start with any kind of meat. It doesn't have to be one of those fancy cuts that has its own name. Most sausage is made from whatever is left on an animal carcass, be it actual muscle or just tendons, connective material, blood vessels, nerves, or bone marrow. Anything goes!

2. Trim the meat you plan to use away from the bone. If you can't trim it away with a knife, various industrial processes will blast the meat away from the bone, producing what is called "mechanically recovered meat." These often involve pureeing the entire carcass and then forcing the slurry through a sieve, separating the bone fragments.

3. Put your meat through a grinder. Or, if you're already working with a meat slurry from a mechanical process, you can skip this step.

4. Add seasonings. Your ground meat or slurry from leftover carcass remnants may not have a lot of flavor on its own. Now is a great time to add some seasonings of your own. Have you tried fennel?

5. While intestines are the most common type of sausage casing, sometimes a stomach or other organ can be used, such as with haggis. Regardless, you need to thoroughly wash your organ casing to make sure any remnants of digested food or excrement are removed.

6. Stuff your ground meat or slurry into the casing, molding it to the size and shape of your choice.

7. Cut the casing and tie it off on both ends to keep your assorted animal remnants from oozing out.

8. Be sure to thoroughly cook your sausage before you eat it; homemade sausage is one of the most common sources of trichinosis reported to the Centers for Disease Control.

HOW TO TOILET TRAIN YOUR CAT

*Face it: Your cat is the ruler of your house.
She knows it, and so do you. So why
shouldn't she sit on the throne?*

WHAT YOU'LL NEED

- Absorbent cat waste material. Clumpable kitty litter will ruin your plumbing, so try an organic or natural kind, or shredded newspaper.

- Cardboard box

- Cat litter

- Plastic to place underneath the cardboard

- Scissors

JAZZ, CATS

In 1968, jazz legend Charles Mingus of all people self-published and sold a pamphlet called "The Charles Mingus CAT-alog for Toilet Training Your Cat." It's the earliest known commercial undertaking of the idea, and the basis for all future thought into the process.

DO IT YOURSELF!

1. Replace your cat's regular litter box with the
    cardboard box, fill it with its familiar litter,
    and leave it in the cat's usual spot. Once she is
    acclimated to these changes—which will take
    a few days—gradually move the box toward
    the bathroom, relocating it by just a few feet
    each day.

2. Once the box is in the bathroom, the pace
    slows down. Move the box to the foot of the

latrine, and then up under its seat, where it should stay for at least a week or two. This is where most training regimes go awry. The inconvenience of moving the pan every time you need to use the bathroom—to say nothing of the gross-out factor—leads many would-be trainers to give up. Patience and persistence are vital.

3. After the first few days, cut a hole in the bottom of the box, gradually enlarging it as time goes on.

4. When the hole is the same size as the area inside a toilet seat, suspend the cat's litter pan under the seat, but over the bowl.

5. The cat must come to feel comfortable on the seat, and only practice will help her achieve the proper balance. Once she gets the idea, though, your cat is likely to take to it thoroughly.

6. Teach your cat how to flush.

HOW TO MAKE CIGARETTES

Smoke 'em if you got 'em...unless they're bad for you or something.

WHAT YOU'LL NEED

- Some good, suitable land for growing crops
- 12 tobacco seeds, preferably of the White Burley variety
- Pots
- Soil
- Scythe
- Pesticides
- Sharp knife
- A barn
- Fire pit
- Firewood
- Industrial shredder
- Shredded paper
- Ammonia
- Nicotine
- Cocoa
- Licorice
- Sugar
- Menthol
- Levulinic acid
- Rolling papers
- Glue
- Filters

BAD SIN-TAX

State with the highest cigarette taxes: New York. Every pack carries an extra $4.35.

DO IT YOURSELF!

1. Buy several acres of land. Not trying to compete with billion-dollar multinational corporations? Then your backyard garden will suffice.

2. If you want enough to smoke, you'll need to grow at least 12 plants. (And since tobacco is one of the most addictive substances on earth, you'll probably want more than that.) Germinate your seeds for a week.

3. Carefully plant the seeds in pots filled with moist, nutrient-rich soil. Let them grow for a month.

4. Transplant the pot, including the dirt and the seedlings, into the land you've set aside for growing tobacco. Water your growing plants and make sure they get a lot of sunlight (you should know that already).

5. Occasionally treat them with pesticides to keep bugs and garden pests away. (Ironically, what's a major ingredient in many pesticides? Tobacco.)

6. Wait several months, until your plants are about five feet tall. Carefully pluck your crop out of the ground and remove all of the leaves.

7. Set up a curing shack. In this barn, keep a fire burning continuously for about a month. Hang the tobacco leaves in here for the entire time to fire-cure them. This will make for a more appetizing, yellow-colored tobacco leaf. (It also increases the amount of carcinogens in the tobacco.)

8. The whole leaf is cured—stems included— because stems, although bitter-tasting and ultimately poor-burning, are rich in nicotine, the addictive substance that gives cigarettes

their kick. To account for that, chop off the stems of the cured leaves, mince them, and set them aside. Take a small portion of the cured tobacco leaf and shred it to make scrap leaf.

9. Combine the minced stems, scrap leaf, and shredded paper, along with a little water and some sugar. Making it into this pulp will make the stems both burn better *and* taste better.

10. Now, add in the ammonia to the pulp. Yes, it's a toxic chemical, but it raises the pH of the tobacco, freeing more of the nicotine to make it more readily absorbable when the tobacco is smoked.

11. Add in small amounts of licorice and cocoa. It won't be enough to impart those specific tastes into the cigarette, but it will make for a better, smoother flavor. They also contain chemical compounds that open airways to allow the lungs to take in more smoke, and thus absorb more nicotine.

12. Add the sugar. This makes smoke easier to inhale. As it burns and reacts to other

chemicals, it forms a chemical called *acetaldehyde*, which makes it easier for the body to absorb the nicotine.

13. Throw in some additional nicotine.

14. Even if you didn't plan on making menthol cigarettes, add some menthol to the pulp. It numbs the throat, reducing irritation caused by inhaling caustic smoke.

15. Toss in some levulinic acid. It's a salt that makes nicotine less harsh and smoking smoother.

16. Allow the ground-up, chemical-treated, tobacco-and-paper pulp to dry. Crumble it, and add in the rest of the tobacco leaf, shredded.

17. Carefully mix up and crumble the mixture and let stand.

18. Place a small amount of the tobacco mixture in a rolling paper. Glue on a filter, and feel alive with pleasure.

HOW TO EMBALM A CORPSE

What to do with that mortal coil when someone shuffles off this mortal coil.

WHAT YOU'LL NEED

- A body
- Plastic apron, gown, surgical cap, gloves
- Respirator
- Porcelain embalming table
- Disinfectant
- Razor, shaving cream
- Needle injector, with wire
- Scalpel
- Medical-grade twine
- Large glass container
- Formaldehyde
- Metaflow, an embalming chemical
- Chroma-tech, a vein-hardening chemical
- Embalming machine (We recommend the Mortech 1036-13 Flush Embalming Station)
- Trocar
- Hydroaspirator
- Tissue fixer
- Syringes
- Glue
- Cotton balls
- Moisturizer
- Makeup

DO IT YOURSELF!

1. Lay the body on the porcelain embalming table in a cold room (the porcelain, like the cold room, stays cold, and slows decay while you work). Put on your respirator, and remove the deceased's clothing, bandages, catheters, leftover medical equipment, jewelry, and any other inorganic objects.

2. Wipe clean with disinfectant the eyes, mouth, all of the various body cavities, and all of the skin, head to toe.

3. The biggest workplace hazard for a mortician: *rigor mortis*, the posthumous stiffening of the limbs and joints. Delay it temporarily by massaging the body's major muscles, and gently move the arms, legs, and head back and forth and all around. Do it gently—things can and will break or pop.

4. Shave the corpse's face, even if it's a woman— all adults have a fine layer of facial hair or fuzz that is barely detectable but can make funeral makeup apply improperly and look strange.

5. The mouth tends to hang open after death, so stuff it with cotton. Then use the "needle injector." It's a metal, gunlike object that shoots a wire into the upper gums. Shoot another wire into the lower gums. Pull the two wires together and twist until the mouth is closed.

6. Cut off any excess wire.

7. It's time to start preparing the inside of the body. Use the scalpel to make an incision on the right clavicle, or collarbone, just above the sternum. The skin flops open, making it easier for you to find the thick, white carotid artery. Tie it off with medical-grade twine to prevent blood from flowing out of the body where and when you don't want.

8. Locate and cut open the jugular vein—that's where the blood will exit the body when it's flushed out with embalming solution.

9. In the glass container, combine the formaldehyde, Metaflow, Chroma-tech, and water. Your embalming chemicals are ready!

10. Pour the mixture into the embalming machine. It looks like a large cylindrical aquarium with a thick plastic tube connected to it. The other end of the tube connects to a thin, L-shaped metal pipe called an "arterial tube," which you'll then insert into the carotid artery.

11. The thick embalming fluid will flow out of the machine, through the tubes, and into the body, where it stays. With nowhere to go, the blood is pushed out of the body through the jugular vein and is washed down the drain.

12. As the fluid flows and fills up the body—it takes between 60 and 90 minutes—once again massage the legs and arms. This ensures that the blood flows out at the proper rate, and none of the embalming fluid gets caught in the body's more narrow passageways.

13. The fluids will temporarily preserve the body (and add lifelike color to the face), so now it's time to tackle the internal organs. Take the trocar, a 2-foot-long metal tube attached to a plastic hose, and the hydro-aspirator. Insert its pointed end into the stomach, just above and to the left of the belly button.

14. Poke around the central body cavity until you've found the spleen, kidneys, and liver. One by one, puncture each with the trocar, and then suck out the organs' internal fluids with the hydro-aspirator.

15. Reverse the hydro-aspirator, and then the trocar pumps in embalming fluid. Repeat for each organ.

16. Fill up the abdominal incision with cotton, and then sew it shut with a "baseball suture" technique—so named because the stitching looks like the stitches on a baseball.

17. Fill the syringe with tissue fixer to plump up the nose, ears, and brow if the dead appears especially emaciated after a long illness. To further preserve facial features, insert cotton balls inside the nasal cavity, eyelids, or mouth.

18. Glue the eyeballs to the eyelids so they stay closed during the funeral.

19. To prevent the body from drying out and looking crusty or flaky at the funeral, use a regular cream-based moisturizer on the face and hands. Also apply makeup to the face, neck, or hands to cover up any visible bruises or lesions.

20. Clothe the body, and place the right hand over the left so the deceased appears at peace.

21. Place the body in a coffin, where it will never be seen again.

BODY OF KNOWLEDGE

• What's the difference between a funeral director, a mortician, and an undertaker? Nothing. The funeral industry prefers "funeral director" because it sounds less ghoulish.

• OSHA regulations require funeral directors to wear respirators while working. Just because a person is dead doesn't mean he or she can't pass on germs.

HOW TO REMOVE YOUR OWN APPENDIX

About 300,000 people report to an emergency room for appendicitis each year. Amateurs!

WHAT YOU'LL NEED

- Alcohol, for sterilization
- Alcohol, for drinking
- Mirror or smartphone
- Scalpel
- Something to sop up the blood
- Surgical needle and thread

DR. DIY

• In 1961, Soviet researcher Dr. Leonid Rogozov diagnosed himself with appendicitis while on an expedition to Antarctica. Because he was the only doctor on staff, he was forced to remove his own appendix. Dr. Rogozov performed the surgery while under a small dose of Novocaine. His crew members assisted him by holding up a small mirror, but he was quoted as saying he worked "mainly by touch." The surgery took just under two hours. He was back to work after only two weeks of recovery time.

• The appendix is a 4-inch tube at the end of the large intestine. What does it do? Your guess is as good as the medical establishment's, which has yet to reach a consensus on the appendix's function.

DO IT YOURSELF!

1. If you have access to the Internet or a library, try to find out as much about the surgery as possible. Most important: the precise location of the appendix, although the throbbing pain in your abdomen is a good place to start hunting.

2. Use the sterilizing alcohol to sterilize your cutting tools.

3. Use the drinking alcohol to get yourself drunk enough to steel yourself to perform major surgery on yourself, but not so drunk that you can't perform the surgery on yourself.

4. Lie down on a comfortable surface where you don't mind spilling some blood.

5. Hold up a mirror (or a smartphone camera) down by where you'll cut, angled so you can see what you're cutting into.

6. Cut into your own skin. And flesh.

7. Reach in and cut out the appendix.

8. Make sure to take breaks every five minutes or so to prevent your death from shock.

9. Once you locate and remove the appendix, dispose of it properly. Cutting open your own belly is no excuse for being a litterbug.

10. Don't forget to sew yourself up!

HOW TO MAKE CANDLES (THE OLD-FASHIONED WAY)

Whether for a romantic dinner for two, or even just to light up the bath while relaxing all alone, candles are a perfect way to set the mood...in a beefy way.

WHAT YOU'LL NEED

- Cow
- Bolt pistol
- Very sharp knife
- Food processor
- Stockpot or slow cooker
- Candlewick
- Clean glass canning jars
- Cheesecloth or pantyhose
- Two pencils
- Colorful ribbon (or other decoration)

A WHALE OF A TAIL

Up until the mid-1800s, beef tallow was the most prominent candle material (in second place: beeswax). By that point in time, the seafaring age had given way to widespread whaling—and candle makers discovered that spermaceti made for great candles. It's a wax found in a whale's head cavity, requiring the whale to be slaughtered.

DO IT YOURSELF!

1. Shoot the cow in the forehead, directly between the ears. (Not between the eyes, or your shot will be too low to hit the brain.) The cow should drop dead immediately.

2. As soon as it hits the ground, cut its throat with a knife, being sure to sever all the main blood vessels. Fully drain the blood from the animal; pumping the foreleg up and down will help drain the blood faster. Don't be alarmed if the cow kicks—these are just unconscious reflexes, and the cow is not still alive and out for revenge.

3. To make the tallow for candles, you'll need fat. Any fat will do, but the best fat for making candles is the fat located around the cow's kidneys. It has a waxy feel and an almost cellophane-like coating. Once you've located it, it should be pretty easy to cut away and remove from the carcass.

4. Trim away any bits of meat, blood, or gristle that may be attached to the fat. Then cut

the fat down into small, uniform chunks. If you have a food processor, run the fat through it until it's the consistency of ground hamburger.

5. Melt the fat: Drop your fat chunks into a stockpot or slow cooker and cook over very low heat. It will take a long time to melt, perhaps as long as six hours. Eventually, the fat will liquefy, and any impurities will rise to the top and get crispy. Warning: Keep that temperature low! Resist the urge to try to speed up the process by raising the heat, or you could end up with burnt fat.

6. Pour the liquefied fat through your cheesecloth or pantyhose into a bowl or some other vessel to strain out all those little floating bits. Once the fat has been strained, allow it to cool but not to harden.

7. Prepare your jar and candlewick: You need to get your candlewick to stand straight in the middle of the jar before you pour your tallow around it. This can be tricky! One technique

is to lay two pencils horizontally over the top of the jar and pinch the candlewick in between.

8. Pour the tallow into the jar: Carefully pour your cooled (but not hardened) beef tallow into the jar, being careful to keep the candlewick in the center of the jar. As the tallow continues to cool, it will eventually harden and, voilà, you've got your candle.

9. Tie a colorful ribbon or attach some other kind of decoration to the outside of your jar. Be creative!

10. Just like that, you've made a homemade candle the old-fashioned way—and your friends are sure to love it. Just be sure to warn them that unlike modern candles, these will smell of burning animal fat as they burn.

11. Tell everybody to call you "Chandler" now— that's the profession name for an old-timey candle maker.

HOW TO MAKE GLUE (THE OLD-FASHIONED WAY)

If you swing by the Back-to-School aisle today and pick up a bottle of Elmer's glue, you'll find an adhesive made entirely of chemicals and synthetic polymers. Maybe that's the right choice for some parents, but many of us prefer our children to be exposed to all-natural products.

WHAT YOU'LL NEED

- Bits of animal hide or other remnants
- Stockpot
- Colander
- Pantyhose or cheesecloth
- Respirator
- Sharp knife

DO IT YOURSELF!

1. Trim your hide and other animal remnants into small pieces. The smaller and more uniform the chunks, the faster your glue will form.

2. Fill your stockpot with water and bring it to a boil. You might want to avoid using your favorite pot, unless you want the soups you make in the future to taste like rotting flesh.

3. Open some windows, turn on a few fans to create a cross-breeze, consider lighting some scented candles, and, if possible, wear a respirator—it's going to get stinky! In fact, if you have access to an old shed or an abandoned house, you may want to make your glue in there.

4. Drop your animal remnants into the boiling water and reduce the heat. Simmer for a few hours, until the hides turn translucent.

5. Pour the mixture through your colander to strain out the large bits of hide.

6. Return the liquid to the stove and continue simmering to boil off all the excess water. Once the mixture begins to thicken, remove it from the heat and allow it to cool.

7. As the liquid cools, test it out. Does it feel sticky? If so, you're almost done, because glue is supposed to be quite sticky.

8. Strain the still-warm liquid through a cheesecloth or even a pair of pantyhose to remove any fine bits that might remain. If you do use pantyhose, be sure it's not a favorite pair; they'll only be good for extremely informal events after this.

9. Allow the liquid to fully cool into a congealed mass. It should feel slightly rubbery, more like rubber cement than Elmer's glue.

10. Break the congealed mass up into small bits and allow it to dry. Now you can store your glue for later use.

11. When it's time to use, mix a few bits of your dried glue with hot water until the bits melt into the desired consistency.

12. Spread your glue on anything you want to stick together, and allow a few *days* to dry.

HOW TO MAKE GELATIN (THE OLD-FASHIONED WAY)

Why buy when you can make it so easily out of hooves and a huge plastic vat?

WHAT YOU'LL NEED

- Many pounds of animal remnants
- Sharp knife
- Surgical-grade bone saw
- Colander or strainer
- Power washer
- Aluminum cauldron
- Roasting pan
- Distilled water
- Two huge plastic vats
- Microwave
- 20 gallons of lime
- 20 gallons of a 4% hydrochloric acid solution
- Cheesecloth
- Food dehydrator
- Food processor
- Kool-Aid mix

DO IT YOURSELF!

1. Gather up any sheep or horse bones, hooves, skin, or any random body tissue you might have lying around (this is a great

way to get rid of any scraps left over from the DIY hamburger experiment on page 118). Don't have any? Don't worry: Call a local slaughterhouse and ask for "raw pre-processing waste." But make sure that the bones and skin they give you are fresh—any more than a day old won't do.

2. Carefully inspect the body parts. Discard any pieces that smell foul or look rotten. Overly decayed bits of bone and flesh produce stringy and inconsistent gelatin. (And besides, they're gross.)

3. Cut the parts into small pieces, about 5 inches wide. Use a sharp paring or serrated knife on the skin and tissue. For the bones, you're probably going to have to use a top-of-the-line electric carving knife, power saw, or surgical bone saw.

4. Place the small pieces in a large colander or strainer. Take everything into the backyard and thoroughly wash the pieces off with a high-pressure hose or power washer. This

will get rid of any unwanted animal debris, such as leftover blood or gristle.

5. Throw the clean pieces of bone, hoof, and tissue into a big pot and soak them in boiling water for about five hours. (The power-washing got rid of the blood and gristle, but a boiling bath gets rid of almost all the fat.) After five hours of boiling, the fat will be floating at the top of the pot. Skim it off and throw it away.

delicious
GELATIN
lime flavored

6. Preheat your oven to 200°F. Place the clean, fat-free bones, skin, and other tissue in a roasting pan and bake for 30 minutes.

7. Back to the backyard. Get a huge plastic vat, fill it with lime, and toss in the animal chunks. This partially decomposes the materials, removing unwanted minerals and organic body chemicals from the body parts. Let it all soak in the lime for about two days.

8. Get another plastic vat and fill it up with a mixture of 96% water and 4% hydrochloric acid (available in any scientific-supply store or on the Internet). This facilitates the release of collagen from the animal material, which is the bouncy "gelatinous" element of gelatin. Leave the pieces in the vat for three days.

9. After removing them from the acid bath (wear gloves!), take the pieces back inside and throw them into an aluminum cauldron and boil them in distilled—not tap—water. Using a slotted spoon, carefully skim off any

• In the modern-day Western world, we don't generally associate meat with desserts…but that's gelatin. Since the 1400s, people have been extracting collagen from the boiled bones and connective tissues of livestock, and adding sweeteners and flavorings to it.

• It wasn't until 1845 that the concept was patented. Peter Cooper registered the idea in 1845 but sold it to a cough syrup company, which then sold it to a high school dropout named Frank Woodward for $450. Woodward created Jell-O, the best (if only) known gelatin dessert manufacturer in the world.

gooey chunks that rise to the surface. This is waterlogged gelatin, and it's what you've been after for the past week.

10. Next, the liquidy gelatin chunks have to be sterilized. In gelatin-processing plants, they go into a high-heat flash heater for four seconds. If you don't have an industrial flash heater, put the goopy bits in the microwave on a ceramic plate (it's soak-proof) for about 10 seconds.

11. Strain the chunks through fine cheesecloth to filter out any tiny remnants of bone, skin, or meat that remain attached to the gelatin.

12. Separate the semisolid gelatin from the liquid by drying it out. Processing plants use the industrial flash heater for this, too, but you can substitute a home food dehydrator or beef-jerky maker lined with wax paper. Let it sit for about 24 hours.

13. You're almost done! Scrape the dry (but slightly sticky) gelatin out of the dehydrator and put it all in a food processor. Grind it into a powder. Mix in some powdered flavorings—Kool-Aid mix works pretty well. Add in the hot water and let it stand in the fridge for a few hours.

HOW TO MAKE A STAINED-GLASS WINDOW

*If artisans could do it in the 13th century,
how tough could it be for you, now?*

WHAT YOU'LL NEED

- A sketchpad, as well as all the drafting supplies you'd find in an architect's office (blueprint paper, a drawing compass, etc.)

- A sheet of graph paper the same size (or larger) as the window you're planning to build

- Several sheets of glass that are at least 1/2-inch thick, from a stained-glass window supplier, in all the colors you'll need for your design

- Glass cutter

- Bottle of cutting oil

- Light box

- Black marker

- Electric glass grinder

- Gemmail adhesive, a glue used specifically in the creation of stained glass

- Enamel solution

- Kiln

DO IT YOURSELF!

1. Make a conceptual sketch of what you'd like your stained-glass window to look like. For the sake of an example, we're going to go with Louise Belcher, the pink bunny hat–wearing troublemaker from the Fox TV show *Bob's Burgers*.

2. Prepare a blueprint that outlines the size of your window and the dimensions of all the scores required for the design. For Louise, you'll need scores for all of the different parts of her face, body, clothes, and bunny hat.

3. Take the graph paper and sketch out a full-scale pattern for your window.

4. Place the pattern on the light box and place your first sheet of glass on top of it. Use the marker to trace the outline of your first score (the pink hat, maybe) and cover the lines in some of the oil. This will make cutting easier.

5. Cut out the score with the glass cutter. Don't stop until you've made the entire cut. If you

do, there's a good chance the glass will break and you'll need to start over with a new sheet. Be gentle but firm with your cuts.

6. Repeat this process until you've got every score you need.

7. With any luck, all the scores will actually fit together. Use the glass grinder to remove the sharp edges and fine-tune them. Be careful! Too much pressure may cause them to chip.

8. Use the adhesive to connect all the scores together.

9. Wait for everything to dry. Then, very carefully, cover your new masterpiece in the enamel solution.

10. Lift the window into the kiln. The heat will further fuse all of the scores together and help make the window stronger.

11. Remove the window from the kiln and wait for it to cool. If you want to adhere to traditional methods, you can now mount the window onto a metal light box.

12. If you're feeling more adventurous—and want to show off your work—remove a window in your home of the same size and replace it with your new creation. With any luck, it won't break into a million pieces and will actually withstand the force of a light breeze.

GLASSY GENTS

• The process of building these windows is the same as it was a thousand years ago, although modern tools and techniques have made it quicker and easier. Cologne Cathedral in Germany installed a 1,200-square-foot window in 2007 made up of 11,500 individual "scores" (the cuts of glass that make up a stained-glass window).

• At various times in history, artisans and craftsmen have used materials like cobalt, bits of iron, and even gold to achieve the colors they wanted.

HOW TO GIVE YOURSELF HAIR PLUGS

Luscious locks lost their luster? You could always try Rogaine, or Propecia, or a hair transplant.

WHAT YOU'LL NEED

- Shampoo
- Antibacterial cream
- Prescription-strength painkiller
- Pot of coffee
- Two microsurgical blades
- Mirror
- Fine-tooth tweezers
- Petri dish
- Saline solution
- Fine-tip permanent marker
- Razor
- Scissors

DO IT YOURSELF!

1. Determine your "donor site." This should be a spot on your head where your hair is still plentiful. Trim the hair in this area down to 1–2 mm in length.

2. Wash your hair with the shampoo, and allow it to dry completely. Then apply the antibacterial cream to your donor site and the area (a.k.a., the "recipient site," or "bald spot") where you'll be inserting the plugs.

3. Draw a series of 1-millimeter dots across the recipient site with the marker for each spot where you'll be inserting a plug of hair. Note: You may need anywhere from several dozen to several thousand dots depending on how much hair you hope to replace.

4. Fill the Petri dish with the saline. (You can also use a regular dish that's just come out of the dishwasher, but make sure that it doesn't have any crusty stuff on it. Hardened cheese is especially bad for hair plugs.)

5. Swallow a few of those painkillers, because this procedure is going to hurt. A lot.

6. Drink the pot of coffee, because those painkillers can make you sleepy, and this is very repetitive, very boring surgery that could make you nod off.

7. Grab your micro-blade and get ready to operate. While relying on the mirror to see what you're doing, make a tiny incision into the first spot in your donor site. Your goal is to obtain a 0.6 to 1 mm graft of hair and tissue.

8. Use the tweezers to remove the graft. Place it in the dish full of saline.

HAIR YOU GO!

• While plugs are the most effective method of hair restoration—they involve taking hair follicles from other parts of the body and surgically implanting them on top of the head—they can run as much as $10,000.

• These days, the most commonly used and effective method of restoring hair via plugs is "follicular unit extraction," or FUE. It tends to create a more natural-looking head of hair and reduces the potential for a spotty or "pluggy" look. This involves removing one to four hairs at a time…along with the nerves, oil glands, and tiny muscles beneath them.

9. Use the second surgical blade to make a "recipient wound" in the first dot in the recipient site.

10. Place the graft into the recipient wound. If it falls out, try again.

11. Repeat steps 6 through 8 hundreds if not thousands of times, until you've filled every dot in the recipient area or you're about to pass out from blood loss, pain, or boredom.

12. With any luck, your new plugs won't become terribly infected and will actually "take." This means that the skin on your head won't reject them, causing the relocated hairs to dry up and fall out. If all goes well, you'll get a head of hair as lush and full as Fabio's, circa 1994.

HAIR TODAY...

In the early 1980s, some doctors discovered a chemical treatment that really did help aid hair growth: estrogen. The female hormone, rubbed directly on the male scalp, was successful at regrowing hair. However, it also cause male test subjects' voices to drop an octave, as well as a reduced libido, and *gynecomastia*, or enlarged male breasts.

HOW TO MAKE A SMARTPHONE

Like Grandpa always said, spending all of your free time mindlessly poking at your phone means more when you made the phone yourself.

WHAT YOU'LL NEED

- Soldering iron
- A set of precision screwdrivers
- Smartphone camera
- Shielding plate
- Back case
- Smartphone screw set
- Metal support brackets
- Logic board
- Home button
- Front case
- Ear speaker
- Vibrator motor
- Smartphone microphone
- Loudspeaker
- Headphone jack
- Wi-Fi antenna
- Smartphone modem
- Trackpad controller
- Multi-band/mode RF transceiver
- Touchscreen glass
- Touchscreen controller
- Power amp
- Processor
- Firmware
- Smartphone battery and power cord
- Laptop computer

DO IT YOURSELF!

1. First, you'll need to gather all the tools and parts. You *could* construct your own logic board and all these gizmos out of raw materials. To keep things (relatively) simple, we'll assume that you're willing to purchase "cannibalized" parts from old smartphones off the Internet or at a local electronics shop.

2. Connect the shielding plate, which helps prevent the interior workings of the phone from doing stuff like frying your brain, to the back case.

3. Attach the logic board to the back case. Then connect one of the metal support brackets to the home button and place it in the hole on the front case.

4. Attach the ear speaker to the top of the front case and the microphone to the bottom. You'll need both of these in case you're over the age of 30 and want to make a phone call instead of just sending a text message.

5. Add the headphone jack, loudspeaker, Wi-Fi antenna, smartphone modem, trackpad controller, home button, and multi-band/mode RF transceiver. Connect all these to the logic board and be sure to use a bracket where applicable.

6. Connect the touchscreen to the front case and the touchscreen controller to the logic board. Do the same for the power amp and the processor.

7. Place the smartphone camera in the back case. Connect it to the logic board. Then stick in the battery.

8. Attach the front case to the back case. If the battery isn't charged already, plug in the phone's power cord and wait a while. If nothing bursts into flames, you're on the right track.

9. If/when the phone actually powers up, use the USB cord to connect it to a laptop and install the firmware. You'll also need to contact a cell provider for a service plan.

10. If all goes accordingly, you'll have a working iPhone-like thing. If not, you may have a potential ticking time bomb on your hands. In either case, you may want to hold the phone away from your head when you send your first text or make your first call.

TOUCH ME

Smartphone glass screens must be virtually indestructible and scratch-resistant, but thin enough so the computer parts inside can respond to touch, and light enough so the phone isn't weighed down. That's why Corning developed Gorilla Glass, made from pure silicon, and combined with aluminum, sodium, and oxygen to make 0.5-mm-thick glass sheets. They're made tough and touch-responsive with a bath 752°F potassium ions.

HOW TO CLEAN A PORCUPINE

Congratulations on your new pet porcupine! We figure you could use some help learning how to bathe a creature that's covered in sharp and pointy objects.

WHAT YOU'LL NEED

- A porcupine
- Porcupine treats: cabbage or clover
- A shower or bathtub with a detachable shower head
- Pet shampoo
- Kitchen gloves
- Thick apron
- Safety goggles
- Pliers
- Bandages
- A hair dryer

STICKY SITUATION

• Porcupines are the third-largest members of the rodent family, behind only beavers and capybaras. That said, they can vary in size. Some porcupines are as small as kittens, whereas members of the largest species, the Cape porcupine, can weigh as much as 66 pounds.

• When it's relaxed, or trying to woo a mate, a porcupine will flatten its quills (which are also called spines) against its body. Your primary concern while cleaning your pet should be to keep it calm so it doesn't stab you with them.

DO IT YOURSELF!

1. A few days before the bath, take your porcupine into the bathroom. The goal is to convince it that bath time isn't something to be feared. Give it treats during each trip. After a few visits, turn on the water so the porcupine grows accustomed to the sounds associated with bathing. Do the same thing with the hair dryer, on a low setting, and point it toward the porcupine. (You're going to use a hair dryer, not a towel, because that wouldn't go well.)

2. On Bath Day, suit up in your protective gear. Remove any loose quills on the porcupine before you lead it back into the bathroom. Stay as calm as possible as you proceed. If you're relaxed, this should help your porcupine stay relaxed as well...and not raise its quills. Fill the bathtub with a few inches of lukewarm water.

3. If the porcupine's quills are still flat and lowered, gently pick it up and slowly lower it toward the bathwater. If it begins to struggle,

quickly return it to the bathroom floor. Wait a while and try again.

4. Once your porcupine is in the tub, and if its quills are still lowered, turn the shower hose to a low setting and thoroughly hose down your pet. Do your best to avoid spraying the porcupine's eyes and ears. Are both you and the porcupine still calm? Then grab the shampoo and gently work it past the quills and down toward your pet's skin.

5. Once the porcupine is thoroughly lathered up, grab the detachable hose, put it on a low setting, and rinse off your pet.

6. Grab the hair dryer and dry off your pet. Afterward, give your porcupine a few more treats as a reward for not trying to kill you.

7. If this all goes terribly wrong, you should know how to best remove a porcupine quill from your skin. Do *not* just try to yank it out— quills have tiny barbs that will cut your skin. Instead, find some pliers, use them to grasp the base of the quill, and swiftly pull it out

in as straight a line as possible. This should prevent the quill from breaking and causing further damage to your body. Make sure the tip was removed with it. If it's still embedded, use a pair of sterilized tweezers to get it out. Then sanitize the wound and bandage it. Check it routinely for signs of infection in the days that follow.

HOW TO CRAFT VIOLIN STRINGS FROM CATGUT

Don't worry, "catgut" is a misnomer. Old instrument strings weren't made out of the guts of cats. They were made out of the guts of sheep.

WHAT YOU'LL NEED

- A sheep
- Various sharp knives
- Various tubs
- Salt
- Piece of wood cane
- Alkaline potash
- Copper thimble
- Bleach
- Hand-cranked string-twisting machine
- Drying frame
- Horse hair
- Soft cloth
- Olive oil
- Dried grass
- Sterling silver wire
- Yardstick

STRING THEORY

Catgut isn't the only traditional string material. In Asia, braided silk was used. In Scandinavia, horse hair was preferred. Western Europe used catgut.

DO IT YOURSELF!

1. Slaughter a sheep. While the animal is still warm, cut it open and remove its intestine, also known as a "casing" or a "set." Doing so while the body is fresh makes it more likely that the blood vessels that go into the casing will be broken off cleanly and not lead to unsightly and dysfunctional "whiskers" on the casing, which can ruin the sound of a string.

2. With a sharp knife, strip all the fat that will be present on the intestines (as well as all the manure that might be). Rinse the intestines under cold running water to get all the impurities off.

3. Soak the intestines in a tub for two days. Remove and salt them.

4. Lay the long, stringy intestines (which are about 60 feet long) on a large, flat, clean, and disinfected surface. With a chunk of wood cane, scrape the outer layers to remove any more remaining fat and/or membranes.

5. Make a solution in a tub of water and alkaline potash. This will soften the intestines.

6. Pull them out of the solution momentarily and rub the length of each intestine against a copper thimble. This serves to scrape away any more fat or waste material that surfaces.

7. Repeat step no. 6 five times a day for seven days. At that point, you'll have pure, nearly translucent muscle.

8. Slice the intestinal ribbons into as many separate ribbons as possible.

9. Cut those ribbons into 23-foot lengths.

10. Bleach all the intestinal sections for four days. This will preserve color and prevent rotting.

11. Take a number of strips, with the number depending on which string you're making. Let's start with the highest, or thinnest, violin string. That will require six sections of intestinal ribbon.

12. Tie all the ribbons' ends together in a loop. Hook it up to a hand-cranked string twisting machine. Twist them together, which will make one very long, tightly wound, single string.

13. Soak the string in water to rehydrate it (twisting it tends to dry it out), and twist again.

14. Hang the string on a drying frame. As it dries, the string will shrink in diameter but grow in length. Over the course of the seven days you'll allow it to dry, remove and retwist on the twisting machine to account for this newfound slack.

15. After a week, the string will be hard, stiff, and slightly yellow in color. It's ready for the final steps. Do not remove it from the drying frame yet. First, rub it with horse hair, which will make the string smooth and give it an even consistency.

16. Polish the string with abrasive dried grass held inside of a soft cloth soaked in olive oil.

17. Cut it off of the drying rack, right before the knots. Cut the string down to its standard length. Again, since we're working with the smallest violin string, that's going to be about 14 inches.

18. Wrap the string in sterling silver wire, which gives it a good sound and a loud tone.

19. Repeat to make the three other violin strings. (Omit the sterling silver wire on the two lowest-note strings.)

20. Thread into violin or fiddle.

21. Defeat the devil in a fiddlin' battle, and claim his golden fiddle as your prize.

GOT THE GUTS?

• "Catgut" may be short for cattlegut, as cattle intestines can also be used to make string. However, "kit" is also an Old English word for "fiddle."

• Until the late 20th century, catgut sutures were common in surgical procedures. Nowadays, synthetics less apt to cause infections are used.

HOW TO MAKE WINE IN PRISON

Don't let your incarceration prevent you from enjoying the finer things, like a glass of wine you made in a toilet.

WHAT YOU'LL NEED

- A few slices of bread (or a few rolls) gone moldy
- Several garbage bags
- One gallon of warm (not hot) water
- 50-75 sugar packets or sugar cubes
- Fruit juice, Kool-Aid packets, fresh tomatoes, or prunes
- Warm blanket
- Straw
- Toilet

THAT'S GRAPE!

- Prison wine is most commonly known, in prison at least, as *pruno*—after its most famous and commonplace source of sugar, prunes.

- Convicted murderer Jarvis Masters sits on death row in San Quentin. In 1992, his poem "Recipe for Prison Pruno" won a PEN Award. In addition to including some poetic phrases, the recipe is reportedly quite accurate.

DO IT YOURSELF!

1. The wine will ultimately be fermented by yeast, but because yeast packets aren't readily available at the commissary, you'll have to get creative. Swipe some bread from the cafeteria. Yes, bread has yeast in it, but way more yeast lives in bread *mold*. Let the bread sit around for a few days until mold forms.

2. When the bread is moldy, it's brewing day. First, you'll need to build a brewing chamber.

It needs to be double or even triple thick. Stick one plastic trash bag inside another, and stick that inside another trash bag.

3. Pour in a gallon of warm water.

4. Add as much fruity material as you can find. This can be anything from leftover fruit juice to orange rinds, raisins, tomatoes, Kool-Aid, even ketchup packets, or a little bit of each— whatever you can salvage from whatever your prison cafeteria may offer. The fermentation process turns sugar into alcohol, so the more sugar or sugar-rich foods and liquids you have, the stronger the wine will be. Throw in about 50 sugar packets or sugar cubes at the beginning, and add a new one every other day or so.

5. Throw in the moldy bread.

6. Seal the bag by knotting it tightly. Run it under hot tap water every day for about 15 minutes and wrap it in a blanket to keep it warm.

7. As the yeast in the bread mold ferments the sugar into alcohol, it creates carbon dioxide as a by-product, and that has to have some way to escape. So ventilate the chamber by cutting a tiny hole in the garbage bags and inserting a straw.

8. Hide your wine (obviously). Three days will produce a slightly alcoholic wine, but wait a week and the wine will ferment into a strong—but horrible-tasting—brew of about 13% alcohol, the higher end of commercially available wine's alcoholic content.

9. When the week is up...keep waiting. You can't drink it quite yet. You have to "shock" the wine to stop the fermentation process. Here's how: Place the bag (be careful of the straw and straw hole) in the toilet bowl. Flush the toilet every few minutes for about an hour to allow the cold water to wash over the outside of the bag, cooling the wine and ending fermentation.

10. Enjoy! Hope you didn't get caught and sent to solitary.

HOW TO MAKE CONDOMS

Make sure to stay safe out there, both while making and using this project's product.

WHAT YOU'LL NEED

- Gallons of liquid latex
- Large industrial tank
- Cylindrical glass mold
- Antifungal and antibacterial solutions
- Potassium laurate
- Zinc oxide
- Sulfur
- Ammonia
- Electronically charged pole
- Spermicidal lubricant
- Aluminum foil
- Vacuum sealer

BE PREPARED

• Condom usage in North America only took off after soldiers, who were given free ones while fighting in World War II, returned home.

• Condom use decreased after the introduction of the Pill in the 1960s, but the outbreak of the HIV/AIDS virus in the 1980s caused new generations to return to the condom as the primary defense against pregnancy and STIs.

DO IT YOURSELF!

1. Fill up a giant tank with gallons of melted-down natural latex. Don't own a large metal industrial tank? Get one. How do you expect to use your final product without impressing anyone by bragging about your large metal industrial tank?

2. Buy cylindrical glass molds that will be dipped into the latex batter. The FDA sets standards for these molds, so you don't have to unzip and design them yourself. If you can't get a glass mold, find *something* that mimics the shape of a cylindrical glass mold.

3. Prepare a solution, mixing the antifungal and antibacterial compounds, potassium laurate, zinc oxide, sulfur, and ammonia. The antifungal and antibacterial compounds protect against fungus and bacteria, of course. The potassium laurate is a stabilizer, the zinc oxide and sulfur will accelerate the solidification of the rubber, and the ammonia is an anticoagulant.

4. Remove the condoms from their molds. Place them in the solution bath and gently wash them. *Do not dry.*

SKIN DEEP

Rubber condoms made their debut in the mid-19th century, replacing ones made out of sheepskin or intestine.

5. Wrap each condom around an electronically charged pole to shock-test it for durability. Please do not test them out on your local Dave & Buster's electric strength-testing game.

6. Carefully put a few drops of lubricant on each condom and you're done!

7. Place each condom into a square made of aluminum foil and close up the package with a vacuum sealer.

8. If you need us to tell you the next step, uh, tell your parents it's time to have "the talk."

HOW TO MAKE A HAMBURGER

From super-duper-extra-mega-deluxe scratch.

WHAT YOU'LL NEED

- A two-year-old steer weighing roughly 1,000 pounds
- Cattle-holding area
- Bolt pistol
- Cow shackles
- Dressing trolley
- Artery- and vein-draining equipment
- Cattle cradle
- Mechanized saws
- Disemboweling tools
- Rotating skinning knives
- Handsaw
- Chemical decontamination bath consisting of water, acetic acid, lactic acid, chlorine, and hydrogen peroxide
- Large freezer
- Butcher knife
- Meat grinder

DO IT YOURSELF!

1. Raise a steer until it's two years old and weighs 1,000 pounds. Of that, 450 pounds will be edible meat.

2. Employ the services of a local beef-processing facility, otherwise known as a slaughterhouse. The cow will stay in a "holding area" for one day. There the cow waits for slaughter and is not allowed to eat in order to reduce manure production. During the day, the cow poops a lot and is given water to maintain its weight.

3. Move the cow to the immobilization area, and immobilize it with a bolt pistol—a pneumatic tool that shoots a bolt against the cow's skull with enough force to render it unconscious. (It's what Anton Chigurr used to kill people in *No Country for Old Men*.)

4. Place the cow into the shackles and hoist it by its hindquarters onto a rail called a dressing trolley. Cut the main arteries and veins and drain the blood into the floor drain. This is

called *exsanguination,* or "deblooding," and it will definitely make the cow no longer alive.

5. While it's still overhead on the dressing trolley, place the cow into the cradle, where the head and feet are removed by mechanized saws.

6. Remove the hide from the carcass with electric rotating skinning knives.

7. Remove the organs. Slice the abdomen from top to bottom, and then loosen and remove those organs by hand.

8. Take the carcass off the carriage and saw it in half lengthwise, through the center of the cow's backbone. The cow is now two "sides" of beef.

9. Wash the sides of any remaining blood and bone dust.

10. Place the beef into the chemical decontamination bath.

11. Put the meat in cold storage, at 32°F. Leave it there to age for a week—it improves the taste.

12. Cut the meat into primal joints (wholesale cuts).

13. Grind the meat into tiny pellets.

14. Form the meat into a patty.

15. Grill to preferred doneness.

16. Add onions, lettuce, tomatoes, and cheese, if desired.

17. Place on a store-bought bun. (Baking them yourself is too much of a hassle.)

BIRTH OF A BURGER

In the early 20th century, hamburgers were a sketchy food—the meat was comprised of second-rate slaughterhouse leftovers, which was ground up to mask flaws. But in 1921, the first fast-food hamburger restaurant opened in Wichita, Kansas: White Castle. It changed the perception of ground beef, as it allowed customers to see their burgers being prepared. (The "white" in the name was no accident—it was picked to imply cleanliness.")

HOW TO MAKE SOY BURGERS

It's easy to make meat-free "burgers"—mash some cooked beans and brown rice, add some spices, and form into patties. But it won't taste like a burger the way a mass-produced soy patty mostly does.

WHAT YOU'LL NEED

- Soybeans
- Food grinder
- Industrial oven
- Extruder
- Hexane, an industrial solvent
- Water
- Vital wheat gluten, used by commercial bakers to enrich bread
- Stockpot
- Mashing tool
- Food dehydrator

SOY WHAT?

Soy protein has virtually no flavor on its own, and it must be rehydrated before eating. But it can absorb up to three times its weight in liquid, and its porous quality gives it the familiar mouth-feel of juicy ground meat.

DO IT YOURSELF!

1. The process begins by transforming the natural goodness of soybeans into TVP, or "textured vegetable protein." Boil the soybeans until they're mushy, and then mash them into a paste.

2. Dry the paste in a food dehydrator. Once it's dry, grind it into a powder.

3. Treat the powder with hexane, which will separate the protein from the fat. The fat is the yellow stuff—discard it, and keep the protein.

4. Superheat the soy protein, which changes it on a molecular level into a fibrous, porous solid.

5. Shoot it out of an extruder in tiny blobs, which expand on contact with air into puffy nuggets.

6. Dry the soy nuggets, resulting in a granola-like substance of little flakes and chunks.

7. Take the vital wheat gluten, add water, knead it into a dough, and rinse under running water to wash away the starch.

8. Combine the vital wheat gluten with the TVP. The result is a dense, chewy substance that's 75 percent protein.

9. Form into patties, and cook them like you would a hamburger.

MEAT YOU THERE

In a commercial veggie burger, wheat gluten provides the body, and TVP provides the texture. Both will pick up the flavor of the liquid in which they are marinated; dried onions, yeast extract, sesame oil, and a dash of liquid smoke give a fresh-off-the-grill flavor. That's what makes it taste like a real hamburger (well, sort of).

HOW TO MAKE A VINYL RECORD

Are you in a cool rock band with a DIY ethic? Then take your DIY to the next level and make your very own records. All you need is a whole bunch of equipment.

WHAT YOU'LL NEED

- 12-inch-wide circle of aluminum
- Sandpaper
- Nitrocellulose lacquer
- Scraper
- Hydraulic puncher
- Digital recording equipment
- Lathe outfitted with a sapphire blade
- Handheld vacuum
- Soap and water
- Tin chloride
- Liquid silver
- Metal alloy
- Nickel solution
- Prying tool
- Labels
- Glue
- Heating chamber
- Polyvinyl chloride pellets
- Hydraulic press
- Record sleeves

SINGLED OUT

45s were seven inches in diameter. They debuted in 1949, just in time to become the main distribution channel of rock 'n' roll singles.

DO IT YOURSELF!

1. To make vinyl records, in this case an LP, you first must make a master record. Take a 12-inch-wide circle of thin aluminum. It will be gritty, so sand it down and polish it until it's smooth.

IT'S A RECORD

LPs (or long play) records spun 33⅓ times per minute. Introduced in 1948, these 12-inch records held about 25 minutes of sound per side. They were made of polyvinyl chloride, or vinyl for short, creating an enduring nickname.

2. Coat the aluminum disk with a veneer of nitrocellulose lacquer, also called cellulose nitrate. Scrape off any excess that isn't part of a thin, uniform layer and discard (or save to make another record later).

3. The lacquer will start to harden right away. Wait until it's fully dry, and then inspect the surface of the lacquer-covered aluminum disk for bumps, scratches, pits, or dirt. If it's not perfect, chip off the lacquer, melt it down, and start over.

4. Using a hydraulic puncher, cut a hole in the center of the master record.

5. The master record just needs one more thing: sound! Record your music and save it as a digital file to a computerized music recording and editing program.

6. Hook your computer up to a digital record-cutting machine called a lathe. As the music plays, it controls a tiny sapphire blade. The blade etches the sound into the disk as one continuous groove.

7. Check your sound levels and adjust if necessary.

8. Vacuum up scrap lacquer as the sapphire etches the groove.

9. Clean the master with soap and water, being careful not to break the darn thing.

10. Spray the master with tin chloride and liquid silver. The tin will help the silver stick to the master. The result: a silver disk with the groove intact.

11. Wash any stray bits of material off the silverized master.

12. Coat the record in a dull metal alloy. This stiffens the disk.

13. Let it dry, and rinse the disk of extra material once more.

14. Immerse the disk in an electro-charged nickel solution. The nickel fuses to silver and settles into the groove.

15. Pry the metal layer off the lacquer disk. Discard the lacquer, and keep the metal. You'll notice that the silver record isn't quite a record—it has ridges instead of grooves. That's because this is a mold (called a stamper) that will be pressed into vinyl to make the grooves on the finished product.

16. Punch a hole in the stamper with a hydraulic hole puncher.

17. Glue on labels.

18. Take a large amount of polyvinyl chloride pellets and melt them into hot rubber disks called biscuits.

19. On the hydraulic press, place a biscuit under the stamper. Apply pressure and heat with the press—about 100 tons of pressure and 380 degrees, to be more precise.

20. The press will mold the biscuit into roughly record shape, but, more important, the groove will be intact.

21. Trim excess off the rubber biscuit.

22. Immerse the disk in cool water to stiffen it.

23. Package the record in a sleeve with your picture.

24. Become a rock star.

WAXING NOSTALGIC

Common until the 1950s, 78s (because they revolved 78 times a minute) held about five minutes of sound, and they were made with shellac. They were very fragile…which is why you don't see too many 78s anymore.

HOW TO BUILD A GREAT PYRAMID

If you're the god-monarch of an ancient civilization—or just want to look like one—there's only one fitting monument to your ego: a pyramid.

WHAT YOU'LL NEED

- Approximately 2.3 million limestone blocks of various sizes, weighing a total of 5.5 million tons

- Granite blocks of various sizes, totaling 8,000 tons

- Gypsum and rubble

- 500,000 tons of mortar

- Tens of thousands of "dedicated workers"

- Stone-working equipment forged from copper

- Wooden cradles large enough for giant stones, outfitted with pulling straps

- Limestone polish (optional)

THE BIG DIG

We're still not 100% sure how the Pyramids were built. They might have been built by slave laborers or skilled artisans, as few as 14,000 full-time workers or as many as 200,000.

DO IT YOURSELF!

1. Mark off a square, level base in the bedrock, about 750 feet per side.

2. Quarry your limestone blocks. Pound wooden wedges into the quarry walls, then soak them with water; as the wood expands, the wedges crack the stone.

3. Shape the blocks. Shoot for cubes in the neighborhood of $2\frac{1}{2}$ tons apiece. This work was probably done with copper implements, so you'll spend as much time sharpening your chisels as using them.

WONDER-FUL

At 480 feet, the Great Pyramid at Giza was the tallest man-made structure in the world for nearly 3,800 years. The smooth outer cladding is long gone, plundered to build mosques and fortresses. But the core has been standing since 2560 BC, weathering sandstorms and massive earthquakes, making it not only the oldest of the Seven Wonders of the Ancient World but also the only one still intact.

4. Transport your blocks to the work site. This may have been done with wooden sledges, but evidence suggests that cradlelike contraptions were fixed to the corners of the blocks, allowing them to be rolled.

5. Build upward and inward at a 51-degree angle. Lay the first couple of courses using simple levers to raise the blocks. History doesn't reliably record how the upper blocks were set, so it's up to you; you might try a series of spiraling ramps, or some sort of primitive crane assembly. In any case, lay the more finished stones on the perimeter, with rougher blocks inside; fill in with rubble and mortar.

6. Lay passageways and chambers with granite blocks as you build, using arched ceilings for maximum structural integrity.

7. Your pyramid's exterior will have a bumpy look. Leave as-is for a rustic effect, or (optionally) surface with angled and polished limestone plates for a seamless, glassy finish.

HOW TO BREW PENICILLIN

Since time immemorial, opportunistic infections could make even a minor injury life-threatening. Tuberculosis was a virtual death sentence, and a bacterial pathogen like the Black Death could bring whole civilizations to their knees. It's hard to overstate just how revolutionary the introduction of penicillin was. Wouldn't it be neat to whip up a batch at home?

WHAT YOU'LL NEED

- Febreze
- Cantaloupe, bread, or citrus fruit
- Medical flasks
- Oven
- Thermometer
- pH testing strips
- Hydrochloric acid
- Water
- Various salts, milk sugars, and chemicals

HOT FUZZ

Most commercially produced penicillin is made using cultures descended from the fuzz on a single rotten cantaloupe found in Cincinnati in 1943. Really.

DO IT YOURSELF!

1. Drug synthesis should take place under sterile conditions, so hose out your garage carefully, and maybe spray some Febreze.

2. You can use cantaloupe mold if you want to be a penicillin traditionalist, or you can also start with a leftover crust of bread, or the peelings from some citrus fruit. Now, wait a few days to get them good and moldy. Once the mold starts to become visible, and then turns from a gray color into a bluish-green, it's time to start the incubation process.

3. Sterilize a medical-grade glass flask. This is pretty easy to do—place it in a regular oven at 315°F degrees for about an hour.

4. Take the moldy bread or moldy fruit, and cut it up into a handful of bite-size pieces. Do not eat. Instead, while wearing rubber gloves, place the moldy food into the sterilized flask. Here, in the flask, you will incubate the mold. Keep the flask at a constant temperature of 70°F...for a week.

5. Sterilize another flask. Pour in 500 mL of cold water, and then dissolve: 44 grams of lactose monohydrate, 25 grams of cornstarch, 3 grams of sodium nitrate, 0.25 gram of magnesium sulfate, 0.5 gram of potassium phosphate, 2.75 grams of glucose monohydrate, 0.044 gram of zinc sulfate, 0.044 gram of manganese sulfate. Fill the flask up to the one-liter line with more water.

6. Test the water's pH. If it's below 5, add hydrochloric acid until the solution has a pH of between 5 and 5.5.

7. Place the moldy food into the solution. Wait another week, and all the chemicals will extract the penicillin spores—they'll float to the top.

8. Strain the penicillin into another sterilized flask. Congratulations! You've got enough crude penicillin to tackle whatever happens during your next shore leave. (Of course, your weird homemade penicillin is probably more damaging to your health.)

HOW TO PUMP YOUR OWN STOMACH

Did you blow forty bucks at Dollar Taco Night?
Get too festive at Oktoberfest? "Accidentally"
swallow some Silly Putty and a Nerf ball?

WHAT YOU'LL NEED

- Two nasogastric tubes, ideally. If you can't get those, a couple of plastic tubes thin and long enough to stretch from your lungs to your stomach.
- Turkey baster
- Olive oil
- Saline solution
- Bucket
- Ipecac syrup, hydrogen peroxide, or another liquid to induce vomiting

PUMP IT UP!

• The medical term for stomach pumping is *gastric lavage*, and the technique dates back, relatively unchanged, to the late 1800s.

• It's only been in the past decade or so that hospitals have become less reliant on the procedure, preferring to treat patients with drugs or more precise methods. That's because there are many potential complications associated with stomach pumping, including intestinal damage and aspiration pneumonia.

DO IT YOURSELF!

1. Coat the tubes in olive oil. This lubricates them so they're easier to jam down into your insides.

2. Say a quick prayer, grab the first tube, and slowly slide it up your nose. Stop once you've threaded it up your nose and down your throat, and you're sure it's reached your lungs. If you aren't choking by this point, that's a good sign, because this tube will help you breathe during the procedure, and prevent you from inhaling any vomit later on.

3. Take the second tube and slide it directly down your throat. Stop when you feel like it has reached your stomach. If you've made it this far, congratulations on your steady hand and ability to suppress your gag reflex—you may have a bright future as a sword swallower. (If this was happening in a hospital, it's at this point that a medical professional would X-ray your sternum to make sure that both tubes are where they need to be.)

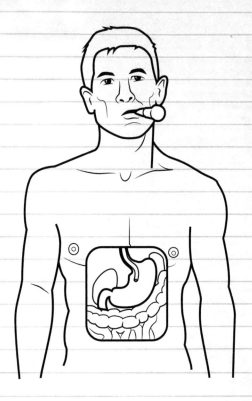

4. Pour saline solution into the tube that leads to your stomach. This will make you feel extremely bloated, even more so than you already are. Once the bloating kicks in, attach the turkey baster into the outside end of the tube, which should still be sticking out of your mouth.

5. It's time to "pump" you up! Squeeze the turkey baster rapidly, shooting air through the tube and into your stomach. This will pull the offending contents of your stomach up through the tube, and, hopefully, out.

6. Once the tube starts to fill with stomach goo, place the tube over the bucket, remove the baster, and allow the contents to flow out.

7. If you were undergoing this procedure in a hospital, now a doctor would likely administer "activated charcoal" to make you regurgitate whatever's remaining in your stomach. Since you probably don't have any of that in your house, use whatever else might help you puke—ipecac syrup or a small amount of hydrogen peroxide, for example.

8. Still alive after all that? Give yourself a pat on the back and get yourself to a hospital as soon as possible to make sure you haven't ruptured anything and aren't facing any further complications in the hours and days to come.

HOW TO MAKE ANTIMATTER

This page is only to be read by interstellar space travelers or supervillains who need a little help building a doomsday device.

WHAT YOU'LL NEED

- Particle collider
- Nuclear physicists
- Construction crew
- Atoms of a high atomic number
- *Lots* of electricity

THIS MATTERS

• Antimatter is a strange material made up of *antiparticles*. They're similar to regular particles, but they have opposite electric and magnetic properties. Scientists believe antimatter could someday be used to power spaceships, cure cancer...or make horrifically destructive weapons.

• The most notable antimatter experiments are currently underway at the Large Hadron Collider (LHC), housed in an underground laboratory in Switzerland.

• In its entire history, the LHC has produced just 10 nanograms of antimatter. That's barely enough to power a 60-watt lightbulb for four hours.

DO IT YOURSELF!

1. This is about the most advanced thing you can do in the world of nuclear physics. So, the first thing you'll want to do is get a degree in nuclear physics. It will (pun intended) matter.

2. Find access to a particle collider. You could put in a few calls to various world governments or contact the European Organization for Nuclear Research. The latter may be willing to part with the LHC for a mere $8 billion.

3. Can't get a particle collider? Then build a particle collider. Pick out a spot 100 miles or so away from civilization, with a circumference of around 17 miles. Then, utilizing more equipment and steps than we can fit into this article, begin drilling into the ground until you reach a depth of 160 feet. Construct a tunnel 15 miles long and 12 feet wide lined with concrete before building the necessary accompanying offices and other facilities. Fill them with all the equipment and nuclear physicists you'll

need, in addition to a few things you may not have considered. WARNING: If you mess up even the smallest thing or miss the tiniest of details, you could maybe destroy the universe. Critics of the LHC argue that its scientists could accidentally create a black hole or a vacuum bubble capable of gobbling up our planet, our galaxy, and all of existence. Plus, privately owning and operating a complex experimental facility like this is likely considered extremely illegal in every country in the world, and doing so might make you the most dangerous human being who has ever lived. However, if you're not the sort of person who sweats the small stuff, gather all of your physicists and get ready to push your collider's "on" button.

4. Check the date on your calendar because making antimatter with your collider could be affected by the moon and what's called "lunar attraction." When the moon is full, the earth's crust rises by about 10 inches. That's enough to really mess with your collider. Wait until a new moon before you hit that "on" button, just to be on the safe side.

5. Construct a "target" comprising atoms with a large atomic number within the collider and hurl some electrons at it. The more energy you use during this process, the more antimatter you'll create.

6. Existing technology makes capturing antimatter and storing it virtually impossible, so, uh, good luck with that. Plus, if you only use your collider to make antimatter and keep it running 'round the clock, after a year you'll wind up with around a billionth of a gram. That means it would take a billion years to create a single gram, and who knows how long to gather enough for a proper doomsday device or a trip to Alpha Centauri. According to a 1999 NASA report, whipping up a gram of antimatter would cost $62.5 trillion.

ANOTHER FUN THING YOU CAN DO WITH YOUR PARTICLE ACCELERATOR

Scientists believe that the big bang occurred about 13.8 billion years ago. This is the theory that the universe started at an extremely hot and dense point, expanded rapidly, and then cooled, allowing the formation of everything, from subatomic particles to stars. A key tenet to the theory is that the universe is still expanding. The theory of an expanding universe was first proposed in 1927 by Belgian priest/astronomer Georges Lemaître, which Albert Einstein called "the most beautiful and satisfactory explanation of creation to which I have ever listened."

The LHC allows scientists to re-create the conditions that existed just after the big bang banged big. If they were actually re-creating the big bang itself, the resulting universe would end all life as we know it in an instant. But since you've now built your own particle collider in theory, you can re-create the big bang yourself, in theory.

HOW TO MAKE MONEY

What if we told you that you could make money at home? With a little know-how, some basic equipment, and no fear of the consequences, you can make thousands, even millions of dollars.

WHAT YOU'LL NEED

- High-quality computer scanner
- Computer
- $20 bills
- Thin white construction paper
- Paper glue
- Laser printer
- Bleach
- Hardening spray
- Finishing spray
- Embedded plastic security strip
- Security thread
- Watermark

COIN OP

Not only fake bills will get you in trouble—so will counterfeit coins, even though they're much harder to make. There's even a 1792 law on the books that made defacing, stealing, or counterfeiting American coins by U.S. Mint employees a crime punishable by death.

DO IT YOURSELF!

1. Amazingly, even moderately priced, off-the-shelf scanners from a big-box retail chain will do a reasonable job; many of these are capable of scanning at up to 800 dpi. Start by scanning the type of money you want to make. Most counterfeiters use a $20 bill—it's a large enough denomination that you won't have to produce too many to be useful, but small and common enough not to arouse much scrutiny when you hand it over.

2. While your consumer-grade scanner will get the job done, consumer-grade paper will not. Real U.S. currency is actually printed on a material made from cotton and linen fibers, more of a cloth than a paper. It's next to impossible to acquire that kind of card stock outside of a rogue nation or organized crime syndicate. You're going to have to treat the thin construction paper card stock to make it seem more fibrous. Carefully glue two pieces of the paper together.

3. Coat the double-thick paper with hardening spray and finishing spray, both of which are available at your neighborhood craft store (the one next to the big-box electronics store).

4. Print the scanned image of the $20 bill onto the paper, making sure to keep the exact dimensions of the paper.

DOLLARS & SENSE

There's just one more obstacle ahead: You can't spend any of it. The Secret Service is extremely dogged in its pursuit of fake currency. Any act of counterfeiting—even a first offense—is a federal felony that can lead to a prison sentence of up to 15 years. Once you begin dropping your new money around town, they will triangulate your location and track you down in short order.

5. Your next challenge is to replicate the advanced security features in today's money, including an embedded plastic security strip, security thread laced throughout, and a watermark.

6. Congratulations—you made money!

HOW TO MAKE MOONSHINE

It's still illegal in the U.S. to manufacture moonshine in one's own residence. Don't try this at home!

WHAT YOU'LL NEED

- 10 pounds of corn
- Burlap sack
- Tubs
- Stockpots
- Water
- Mashing tool
- Yeast
- 5-gallon jug
- Steel still
- Plastic wrap
- Rubber band
- Cheesecloth
- Mason jars or oak barrels

GOODNIGHT, MOONSHINE

- *Moonshine* gets its name from the light of the moon reflecting off the rivers that smugglers would travel on to sell their contraband liquor.

- The manufacturing of moonshine had its biggest boom in the United States during the Prohibition era (1920–1933).

DO IT YOURSELF!

1. Put the corn kernels into a burlap sack and soak it in a tub of warm water for 10 days. (Burlap sacks are inherently the most devious sacks.)

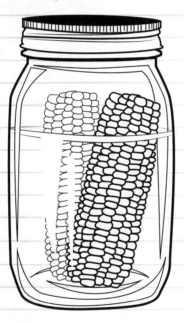

2. Once your kernels have begun sprouting, wash and move them to a large stockpot. Pour in 5 gallons of water and begin to mash up the kernels. Boil it and add in yeast.

3. Pour your disgusting mix into a 5-gallon jug (ideally, one that has "XXX" on the side). Seal the top with plastic wrap and a rubber band so the fermentation process can begin. Wait one week. If you cannot go one week without drinking, get some help.

4. To start the distillation process, you'll need to buy or build a steel still.

5. Use a cheesecloth to filter your fermented muck, which is called the "wash," as in, "You'll need to wash your clothes if you spill week-old corn goo on yourself."

6. Boil the wash to 120–140°F. Once it reaches that temperature, add in cooling water. Liquid will begin to drip out of the condenser. Throw out the first ½ cup that drips out because it's the "head" and does not taste good. But you're drinking homemade moonshine, so taste probably isn't high on your list of priorities.

7. Once your mix reaches 180°F, it's time to start collecting! This is the good stuff. When your mix gets hotter than 200°F, you can stop collecting.

8. Age your moonshine for three months in glass mason jars if you're a hipster, or in wooden oak barrels if you like your whiskey to not taste like garbage.

9. Once it's been properly aged, dilute your product with water to get it to the familiar 40–50% alcohol level seen in store-bought whiskey—and enjoy!

CORNOGRAPHIC MATERIAL

• The alcohol content of moonshine varies, but it's not uncommon to find some in the 70–90% range if not diluted.

• The first major crisis faced by President George Washington was the Whiskey Rebellion, in which Pennsylvanian farmers protested a new tax on homemade distilled liquor. After tax collectors were tarred and feathered, Washington personally led 13,000 militiamen who swiftly squashed the rebellion with little violence.

HOW TO CREATE THE WORLD'S LARGEST DIAMOND

Are you tired of diamonds that won't injure your spine if you tried to wear them on a necklace? Then you might want to try making the biggest one on the planet. (Warning: this is not technically possible.)

WHAT YOU'LL NEED

- Advanced degree in engineering
- Drafting table and various office supplies
- Army of highly trained engineers and construction workers
- BARS apparatus
- Plot of land of at least one square mile
- Power plant
- Several hundred pounds of graphite
- Crane
- Tens of thousands of gallons of oil
- Billions of dollars

MAN OF STEEL

As he's demonstrated in comic books and movies, Superman can squeeze a lump of coal and turn it into a diamond. Doing this is theoretically impossible. Converting raw materials into a gemstone requires not just extreme pressure but extreme heat, about 2,200°F.

DO IT YOURSELF!

1. There are a few different ways to create synthetic diamonds, but the process we'll outline is called "high pressure, high temperature" (or HPHT for short). First, you'll need to build your own BARS apparatus. These devices are considered the most compact, efficient, and cheapest diamond presses around, but they're only capable of creating gems that weigh a measly gram or so. You'll need a much more powerful and much larger BARS (the acronym is short for a Russian geological phrase). Begin by earning an advanced degree in engineering.

2. If you're going to beat the Cullinan diamond, you'll need to design a gem that weighs over 1.37 pounds. To make the math easier, let's aim for a two-pounder. Constructing a BARS apparatus capable of pulling off this task is pretty much impossible (given current technology), but you're not going to let that stop you, right? Grab your drafting table and get ready to make a blueprint.

3. The length of the average BARS apparatus is about six feet. To make a two-pound diamond, you'll need an apparatus that's roughly 900 times larger. Once you're done with your blueprint, you should be looking at plans for a device that's over a mile long and 270 stories tall. In other words, that's going to be the largest man-made structure on Earth.

4. Gather all your engineers and construction workers. Clear all the flora and fauna off your plot and host a groundbreaking ceremony. Then prepare your crew for a substantial amount of

frustration and setbacks. This step is likely to cost you untold billions of dollars and anywhere from 10 to 50 years depending on weather conditions, unavoidable labor disputes, technological advancements, and the project's inevitably destructive effects on your own sanity.

5. Once your gigantic BARS apparatus has been constructed, ride the elevator to the top of it and instruct your crew to use the crane to lower the graphite into its inner chamber. It will serve as what's called a "diamond seed."

6. Fill the chamber with tens of thousands of gallons of oil. By now, you should have the apparatus connected directly to a nearby power plant or an independent, dedicated power source, because you're going to need a *lot* of electricity for what happens next.

7. Press the "on" button. If the BARS apparatus hasn't exploded, that's a good sign. Close the lid and wait for the inner chamber to heat up to a toasty 2,200°F.

8. The apparatus will then apply an immense amount of pressure to the graphite. Kick back and relax, because "cooking" your new diamond could take up to 100 hours.

9. If the apparatus holds together and doesn't wind up flooding the surrounding area with boiling oil, wait for the interior to cool, and then pop open the lid. Have the crew use the crane to bring your new diamond to the top.

10. Clean the diamond off with a napkin or a hankie. Enjoy this moment, because you've achieved the impossible. Despite the immense amount of effort, money, and time, you've poured into this project, your diamond probably won't earn you more than a few hundred thousand bucks. Synthetic diamonds don't sell for nearly as much as their natural counterparts.

SHINE ON

• Humans have been infatuated with these glittery rocks throughout much of history. Anthropologists theorize that they may have been used as engraving tools as far back as 6000 BC. Ancient civilizations in India were among the first to use them as adornments and started adding them to religious artifacts around 4000 BC.

• Because diamonds are the hardest natural material on the planet, they're great for stuff like drilling and cutting other materials. Annually, 30% of all harvested diamonds are declared "gem quality," while the remaining 70% are set aside for industrial applications.

HOW TO MAKE BLEACH

WHAT YOU'LL NEED

- Water
- A thick plastic bottle
- Pool shock, a chemical with calcium hypochlorite at 78% "chlorine yield"

DO IT YOURSELF!

1. Dissolve a heaping tablespoon of pool shock into two gallons of water. This makes a "bleach stock," which you can use as a water purification solution. Add one part of concentrate for every 100 parts of water to disinfect. (To purify a gallon of water, use 1.28 ounces of stock.) To make water drinkable, mix the stock in dirty water and let sit for 30 minutes. If the water is still cloudy, add a little more concentrate. Otherwise, it's ready to drink.

2. To make a big jug of cleaning-grade bleach, add a heaping tablespoon of pool shock to a cup of water. This will make a 5% bleach solution. To get a gallon of bleach out of that, add a tablespoon of this stock to a gallon of water.

HOW TO MAKE A LASER

Step one: make a laser. Step two: point it at the sun...
unless your demands are met.

WHAT YOU'LL NEED

- Laser diode
- Laser housing
- Soldering iron
- Electrical pins
- Drill

- Mini flashlight, including a tiny light bulb and plastic reflector
- Batteries

PEW! PEW!

- Lasers are used for a variety of actions, including reading optical disks, scanning bar codes, advanced weapon targeting, eye surgery, visual effects, and hair removal.

- The high-energy laser weapon commonly seen in movies is now a reality. The U.S. military has multiple laser weapons in development that have successfully destroyed large targets like missiles.

- Charles Hard Townes won the 1964 Nobel Prize in Physics for building the maser, the precursor of the laser.

DO IT YOURSELF!

1. Procure a laser diode, the glowing source of energy that is the visible part of a laser. This is not terribly hard to find—anything that uses a laser has a laser diode. You could remove one from any electronic device you own that reads disks, for example, such as from that CD player you haven't used in a while. If you want a relatively powerful laser, use the diode from a rewritable DVD drive (or DVD burner). It's capable of etching digital material into disks...and can also shine a light hot enough to pop a balloon.

2. Get a laser housing. The housing is a bullet-esque part that will serve as the casing for your diode. If you're a hunter, you can recycle a spent shotgun shell casing. An empty lipstick tube would work, too.

3. Install the diode into the casing. Solder two pins to the positive and negative terminals of the diode.

4. Take a cheap mini flashlight and remove the bulb.

5. Drill a hole in the plastic reflector small enough for your casing to fit snugly inside. Insert batteries so your new laser pointer becomes warm *and* snuggly.

6. Try out your new laser pointer. Take over the world, play real-life *Tron*, or what have you.

LASER POINTS

• In 2011, a 14-year-old boy was arrested for shining a laser pointer into the cockpit of an airplane landing at Los Angeles International Airport.

• In 2014, Detroit Lions fan Mark Beslach was banned for life from Ford Field after repeatedly shining a laser pointer at an opposing team's quarterback...and then bragging about it on Twitter.

• The first item sold on eBay was a broken laser pointer. Company founder Pierre Omidyar got $14.83 for it, although he would've let the buyer back out if he wanted to. The new owner said it was fine because he was "a collector of broken laser pointers."

HOW TO MAKE BIODIESEL

Do the right thing for the planet, and fuel up your car with biodiesel. Or go one better and cut down on the carbon footprint of somebody having to ship the biodiesel to your local gas station.

WHAT YOU'LL NEED

- A liter of new, clean, unused vegetable oil, preferably canola, corn, or sunflower

- 3.5 grams of sodium hydroxide, also known as lye

- 200 ml of methanol

- A glass blender with a low-speed option

- Dutch oven

- Thermometer

- Safety glasses

- Chemical-resistant gloves

- Heavy-duty apron

CORN FUELED

• If your car runs on diesel fuel, it can run on biodiesel—everything from a 1997 Honda Accord to a brand-new Rolls-Royce.

• The U.S. produced 1.8 billion gallons of biodiesel fuel in 2013, up from just 700 million gallons in 2008. Studies have shown that biodiesel fuels reduce net carbon dioxide emissions up to 78%, versus petroleum-based diesel fuel.

DO IT YOURSELF!

1. Pour the methanol into the glass blender. *Do not make margaritas for a robot.* Instead, add the lye and set the blender to a low speed. Let the chemicals mix until the lye has completely dissolved. The mixture has now become sodium methoxide.

2. As the methanol and lye mix, heat the vegetable oil in the Dutch oven until it reaches a temperature of 130°F.

3. Quickly add the oil into the blending chemicals. Continue to blend the mixture on low for another 25 minutes.

4. At that point, the mixture will have separated into two layers: glycerin and biodiesel. The biodiesel is less dense, so that's the stuff floating on top.

5. Allow the layers to rest undisturbed in the blender for 12 to 24 hours.

6. Carefully remove the top layer, and set aside. This is just glycerin. It's nontoxic, so you can

throw it away. Or you can keep it, if you've got some use for some free glycerin.

7. Take your fuel, power up your car, and drive to a forest to hug some trees, you earth crusader, you.

BIO-GRAPHY

• Unlike petroleum-based fuels, the ingredients used to produce biodiesel are renewable. As long as there is corn, sunflowers, and rapeseed, we'll have corn oil, sunflower oil, and canola oil, respectively.

• Biodiesel fuel is most commonly made from vegetable oil or animal fat, but it can also be produced from algae and sewage sludge. But if you want to keep your car running correctly, as well as to keep unnecessary maintenance at bay, it's best to stick with biodiesel made from brand-new canola oil, as opposed to homemade biodiesel, or sewage sludge. (Plus, we didn't tell you how to make car gas from sewage sludge. We don't know how to do that. Frankly, we don't want to know.)

HOW TO FLY TO THE MOON

NASA's plans to get something into space take too much time, employees, and money. It's a lot easier to try it with the plans laid out by Jules Verne in his classic 1865 science fiction novel From the Earth to the Moon: *Just shoot yourself out of a cannon.*

WHAT YOU'LL NEED

- A wide-open space
- Excavation equipment
- Several thousand pounds of cast iron
- Several thousand pounds of liquid steel
- 120 metric tons of gun cotton
- A 1,000-foot wick
- Lots of aluminum
- Seats
- Straps
- Oxygen tanks
- Hydraulic shock absorbers
- Space suit
- Crane
- Matches

HEY, VERNE!

In writing his novel about an attempt to launch a space capsule to orbit the Moon, Verne accurately calculated the Earth's escape velocity. For an object to leave the planet and evade gravity, it would have to travel at a rate of about 11 kilometers per second.

DO IT YOURSELF!

1. Find a spot that isn't densely populated with buildings and where you can dig a really big hole—the cannon you'll make will be so powerful that the only thing you can use to stabilize it will be the Earth itself.

2. Using industrial excavation equipment, dig a hole that's 60 feet wide...and 900 feet deep. (That's about as deep as Lake Michigan.)

3. In the center of the chasm, create a borehole by placing in the middle a cast-iron column the length of the hole. That will be the cannon.

4. Fill in the hole—around the borehole, not inside of it—with liquid steel.

5. Into the borehole, dump about 120 metric tons (roughly 270,000 pounds) of gun cotton. Also known as cellulose nitrate or flash powder, gun cotton was a mid-19th-century technological breakthrough. It provides four times the explosive charge of gunpowder.

Stuff it in there well, so it's as tightly packed as possible.

6. String into the gun cotton a wick—900 feet, plus another 100 or so to hang out the edge, on the Earth's surface.

7. Now it's time to make the space capsule. In Verne's novel, it was constructed of aluminum with walls just 0.3 meter thick, about a foot.

8. Because this space capsule will be driven by an initial explosive rather than by rocket fuel, electricity, or anything like that, no control panels are necessary. But it would be wise to include seats, straps, and an oxygen tank.

9. Outfit the capsule with hydraulic shock absorbers to account for G-force during acceleration.

10. Put on your space suit, get inside the capsule, and make sure the door is closed and airtight.

11. Have a friend use a crane to haul the capsule up and atop the subterranean cannon. Make sure to aim the capsule at the Moon.

12. Have your friend light the wick.

13. Blast off into outer space!

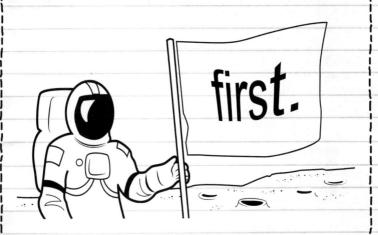

HOW TO CURE A DISEASE

Each year, scientists around the globe fight to find cures for the diseases that ail us. It's a laborious process that requires lots of resources. Want to try your hand at defeating the germ menace?

WHAT YOU'LL NEED

- Money—somewhere between $500 and $2 billion ought to be enough
- Cutting-edge medical research lab
- Dedicated team of biochemists
- Strains of the disease you're attempting to cure
- Protective gear for your scientists if the disease is highly communicable
- Animal test subjects
- Human test subjects

LICENSED TO ILL

Many diseases perpetually evolve and come in a variety of strains. This is why there's no cure for cancer—there's no single kind of cancer. The field of molecular biology has only been around since the 1930s, and there's still much to be learned about how many diseases develop and infect us. Sequencing genomes, studying genes, tracking DNA damage, and other tactics used to find cures constitutes a process that can take years or even decades.

DO IT YOURSELF!

1. Assemble your team, put together a work schedule, and get everything rolling down at the lab. Your team will need to spend the coming months studying the disease, watching how it develops and spreads, etc. If the disease is communicable in animals like rats or guinea pigs, you'll want to infect them with it and observe its impact on their bodies, cells, and DNA. This is all a part of what's called the "preclinical phase" of drug development.

2. Once you know more about the disease and how it operates, you'll want to move on to what's called "high throughput screening." This process involves basically rounding up a bunch of medicinal chemicals and flinging them at disease samples to see what impacts them and what doesn't. If that's getting you nowhere slow, try plant-derived treatments that have been proved effective against similar diseases. If those aren't working, arrange a field trip to the nearest ocean and round up some marine invertebrates. Several drugs have been created by studying the cell structures of sea sponges and snails.

3. Months, years, or even decades may pass as your team continues to search for a cure. As time whizzes by, keep an eye on the pharmaceutical industry. You'll want to make sure that a company like Pfizer or Johnson & Johnson doesn't beat you to the punch and come up with a cure before you do. Once you've got a drug that's working in the lab, it's time to move on to step #4.

ILL COMMUNICATION

The common cold has proved notoriously difficult for scientists to cure. There are many strains, and they're constantly changing. As a trip to your local pharmacy will prove, lots of drugs can relieve cold symptoms. They can stop some of your aches and make your nose a bit less drippy, but they can't get rid of the bug entirely.

4. Now it's time for the "clinical phase," which typically consists of three "trials." This is where your human test subjects come in.

During the phase I trials, give your drug to some healthy people. If they don't die, develop X-Men-like powers, or grow horns, move on to phase II.

5. Give your drug to a small group of patients who actually have the disease. Did it cure them? Awesome! For phase III, pass the drug along to a larger group. Did it work on all, most, or even just some of them? Fantastic!

6. If your drug has a good safety record, meets toxicity standards, and has been proven not to cause any long-term problems or other issues, you'll need to send it off for marketing approval in any country where you plan to sell it. In the U.S., this process is called NDA ("New Drug Approval"), and it can take anywhere from 6 to 10 months in most circumstances. Your drug and application will be thoroughly checked by the Food and Drug Administration before it can be mass-produced, marketed, and shipped off to various clinics and drugstores around the country.

HOW TO MAKE YOUR OWN DENTURES

Afraid of going to the dentist?
Then skip the dentist!

WHAT YOU'LL NEED

- Dental impression trays (plastic or stainless steel)
- Sodium alginate
- Ultracel (dental stone)
- Releasing agent
- Self-cure acrylic powder
- Rotary grinding and cutting tool with sanding cylinder, cutting bits, and felt cone for polishing
- Clay sculptors' tools
- Clay
- Small bowls
- Mixing spoon
- Paint and glue brushes
- Measuring spoons
- Rubber gloves
- Mirror
- Toothpaste, toothbrush, floss, mouthwash
- Pressure cooker
- Lighter
- Wax

DO IT YOURSELF!

1. Test your materials. The alginate and dental stone typically mix with water, and the acrylic powders combine with the monomer like an epoxy. The correct mixing ratios should be specified on the packages or other documentation, but make sure to do a test mix using a small amount of each of the materials with your timer or stopwatch beforehand so you can be sure of their setting times. And it's possible that you may want to adjust the mix ratios for workable consistency.

THE TOOTH HURTS

Although fabricating false teeth may seem more like a craft than a science, keep in mind that most of what you pay for at a denturist is expertise in creating a one-of-a-kind handmade product. And even if you do a really good job making yourself a useful set of teeth, that in no way indicates a talent for making them for others.

2. Clean your teeth well. Floss, brush, and use a mouth rinse.

3. Make the alginate impressions. This is the most important part, and it's probably the step you will have to go back to if you mess up subsequent processes. Fill one of the trays with alginate, and place it into your mouth so it fits properly. There should be a little space all around the teeth and extending beyond the back molars.

THE HARD TOOTH

Getting the materials might be the trickiest part of the process. If you try to place an order with a dental supply company, they'll ask the name of your practice. So who can supply the materials for the denture hobbyist? Theatrical costume and makeup artists often need to make fake teeth in small quantities, so shop where they shop.

4. Even if you intend to create an appliance for only upper or only lower use, make impressions and castings of both—you will want the other one for "bite reference," or to form some teeth later on.

5. Let the trays sit in your mouth for about five minutes and try not to gag. Breathe through

your nose, and relax your jaw and cheeks (a dentist would tell you to do this). Tensed muscles in these areas can result in an inaccurate impression.

6. Remove the impressions.

7. Prepare the Ultracel, and then pour it into the cast you've just removed from your mouth. Check for any air bubbles, and remove them by gently tapping the cast on a table, allowing the Ultracel to flow into all areas. Let it set for an hour.

8. Very carefully separate the cast from the tray—you don't want to damage the plaster.

9. Using the power dental tools, carve away the excess material until you've carved what looks like a uniform set of teeth.

10. These aren't your new dentures—they're the model for them. Now set the plaster teeth upright, with the teeth facing upward. Melt a thin layer of wax onto the plaster.

11. Once again with the sculpting tools, continue to form the fake teeth so they look like real teeth (or real fake teeth).

12. Use a lighter to melt the surface of the teeth just a little bit. This will create a natural-looking smooth finish.

13. Place some clay atop the gum line.

14. Mix up some more alginate in a large bowl. Place the entire melted, waxed, shined cast into it. Hold it in there until it dries, and then remove.

15. Clean all that gunk off your hands and then use your dental tools to gently chip away excess material. Make sure to get any leftover wax.

16. Paint a thin layer of release agent on the cast. Let it dry. Now do that twice more.

17. Place a few drops of acrylic into the mold and move it around so it disperses. Sprinkle acrylic powder into the teeth mold; this will provide a more natural color.

18. Place the plaster teeth into the mold so they fit tightly. Put a weight or some books on it to hold it in place for about 10 minutes.

19. Fill the pressure cooker with water, heat it up, and place the mold inside. Leave it there for 15 minutes and then remove.

20. Carefully separate the molds, remove the plastic teeth from the cast, and chip away any remaining excess plastic.

21. Polish the teeth with a toothbrush and toothpaste…as if they were real.

HOW TO MAKE CROP CIRCLES

Step one: Be an alien. Just kidding. All it takes is a few simple tools and the desire to spook the world.

WHAT YOU'LL NEED

- Large wooden planks of various lengths
- Drill
- Paper and pens for design
- Rope
- Spirograph (optional)
- Measuring tape
- A healthy barley, corn, or wheat field

DO IT YOURSELF!

1. Drill a hole through each end of the plank. String rope through the hole and tie it on each side to make what looks like an old-timey backyard swing.

2. Come up with a design to scale. Classic crop circle designs are elementary geometry: lots of circles and straight lines. However, the more complex you get, the more people you'll

fool into thinking an alien craft landed in the field. If you aren't creatively inclined, get an old children's Spirograph toy off eBay and use the drawings it makes as an inspiration.

3. Measure out and plan your designs in the field as best you can in the dark. (You'll want to do it in the dark. Bower and Chorley evaded detection for years—and made people think aliens were responsible—simply because they worked under the cover of night.)

4. With the rope around your neck, walk forward while stepping on the plank. The pressure of your feet, and the evenness of the rope-held wood, will tamp down the corn or wheat.

5. Continue to do so, following your schematic, until you've created weird, alien-esque field art. Substitute different-sized planks to achieve different design elements.

6. Get out of there before the sun rises.

HOW "THEY" MADE CROP CIRCLES

One Friday night in the late 1970s, Doug Bower met with his friend Dave Chorley at a pub in rural England. The talk turned to the mysterious circular depressions that Bower had seen in cornfields during the eight years he lived in Australia. Some locals speculated that the circles were left by UFOs or aliens, and they were some kind of map or diagram. Bower and Chorley didn't think so—they figured they were a prank.

After a few more drinks, they decided to play the prank themselves. They kept doing it every Friday night, and eventually, folks started noticing. And getting totally freaked out. The story spread nationwide, and then worldwide, and then suddenly there were so-called experts writing books about the symbolism of the circles and what those messages from the aliens meant.

But only Bower and Chorley knew the truth. In fact, Bower's wife didn't even know until she accused him of having an affair. He had put so many miles on his car during Friday nights that she grew suspicious. In 1991, Bower and Chorley let the whole world in on their secret by revealing their story and methods to reporters. Despite Bower and Chorley's admissions, many conspiracy theorists still believe that crop circles are purposeful messages left behind by visiting aliens, or accidental imprints left by enormous spaceships.

HOW TO BUILD A ROLLER COASTER

If you survive the high admission price of the average theme park, you'll live to get vomited on by some kid on a roller coaster who can't handle the awesome twists and turns. Why put up with that when you can enjoy the same thrills in your own backyard?

WHAT YOU'LL NEED

- Sketchpad
- Office supplies you'd find in an engineer's office, like blueprint paper, a drawing compass, etc.
- A backyard or plot of land large enough for a roller coaster
- Building and safety permits
- Metal beams
- Welding tools
- Cement
- Cement mixer
- A shovel
- A ladder
- Welding equipment
- 500 pounds of sandbags
- Track
- Riding cart
- Safety helmet, pads
- Test dummy
- Hay bales (optional)

DO IT YOURSELF!

1. First, design your coaster. If you don't know how to do that, enroll in the nearest college with an engineering program. Barring that, pick up a copy of the PC amusement park simulator game *Roller Coaster Tycoon*. At any rate, when you make your real coaster, for the sake of ease, you'll want to leave out "corkscrews," "headchoppers," and other elaborate features you'd find on a coaster at Six Flags or the like. Keep your coaster realistic and relatively simple. For example, instead of a lift hill with a motorized chain that will pull the cart to the top, scribble in a staircase and a gravity-powered drop hill at the beginning of the track.

BEST COAST

In the early 2000s, a man named John Ivers built the Blue Flash outside of his house in Bruceville, Indiana. The 24-second thrill ride features a loop and is one of the most ambitious backyard roller coasters ever constructed. Ivers even put together a second, tamer coaster for his young grandkids in 2014, the Blue Too.

2. Also: How will your cart stop once it reaches the end? You could conclude the ride with a flat track and allow friction and physics to slow the cart. If you're the more adventurous type, you could toss in some hay bales that the cart will slam into. Brakes?! Who needs brakes?!

3. Sketch out your design in great detail with a CAD program, or draw it yourself and make up some blueprints.

4. File and receive all necessary permits with your city, county, state, or other municipal authority.

5. Break ground! Grab the shovel and dig some holes in your backyard for the coaster's support beams. Once they're in place, fill the remaining space in each hole with cement. Wait for it to dry.

6. Next, grab the ladder, add some crossbeams, and weld them to the support beams.

7. Lay down the track. Place the sandbags at various points along the track to make sure it's strong enough to support the weight of both the cart and an adult rider.

8. Here's where the fun begins. Place the cart at the top of the first drop hill and toss in the sandbags. They'll serve as your crash-test dummy. Push the cart down the track. Did it make it all the way to the end? Congratulations! If not, have a look at the spot where the cart fell off the track and fix it. Keep tweaking the coaster until the cart makes it safely all the way to the end.

9. Next, find a volunteer willing to risk his life on your new roller coaster, preferably the biggest and tallest person you know. Have him put on the helmet and pads before you send him hurtling down the track. Did he survive? Awesome!

DEATH DERBY

Your roller coaster will be not that much different than one built 100 years ago, by people who knew about as much about roller coasters as you do. In 1911, the Derby Racer was built in Revere, Massachusetts, one of the first-ever wooden roller coasters. Just days after it opened, a man was flown from the coaster's signature "figure 8" track, and died. The Derby Racer was closed down and demolished in 1936... after it killed two more people.

10. Once your coaster seems safe enough for you to actually try it yourself, climb aboard. Have fun riding it while screaming at the top of your lungs...until your neighbors inevitably report you to the authorities for noise violations. There's also a good chance a building inspector might show up to make sure everything's up to code.

HOW TO DIG A SWIMMING POOL IN YOUR BACKYARD

It's a hot day, but the nearest public pool is filled with snotty teenagers, and that snooty country club rejected your application. Show them all and build a pool in your backyard. How hard could it be?

WHAT YOU'LL NEED

- Sketch or blueprint
- Backhoe
- Wall supports
- Pipe and filtration system
- Rebar and wood
- Power line
- Water supply line
- Pool lights
- Concrete
- Cinder blocks
- Filtration system
- Swimming pool tiles

- Filling material
- Mortar and various building tools and supplies
- Frozen turkey
- Chlorine
- Water slide, pool noodles, diving board, swimsuit (optional)

DIVING IN

The oldest known concrete pool in the U.S.: the Deep Eddy Pool, built in 1915 in Austin, Texas, and still open for business.

DO IT YOURSELF!

1. First, figure out how big you want your swimming pool to be (and if you can actually fit one in your backyard). Decide and plan now if you want to include a diving board or a water slide. (Of *course* you want to include a diving board or a water slide.)

2. Prepare a sketch with all the schematics. Feel free to do this on a napkin, but a more refined blueprint will likely come in handy at some point.

3. Before you break ground, you'll want to contact your local "smart digging" organization to make sure you're not going to rupture any underground utility lines. If there are pipes or wires running through your yard, you'll need to find another way to cool off. You may also need to acquire various city permits before you get to work.

4. Now it's time to start digging. You could use a shovel, but that will increase your workload tremendously. You're better off using a

POOLS RULE!

• Ancient Greeks and Romans used pools for everything from military exercises to athletic training. The Japanese were the first to turn swimming into a sport, and they hosted competitive races as early as 36 BC.

• The world's first swimming pool was (probably) "the Great Bath." It was located in an urban settlement called Mohenjo-daro in what is now Pakistan. Archaeologists estimate that the pool was constructed anywhere from 4,500 to 5,000 years ago. It measured 39 by 23 feet and was lined with bricks and a tar-based sealant.

• The first ocean liner with an onboard pool was the White Star Line's *Adriatic*, which had its maiden voyage in 1907.

backhoe. They're way more fun to work with, too. Once the hole is in place, grade the floor and walls inside so that they're nice and smooth.

5. Get rid of all the dirt. Your neighbors might get annoyed if you dump it in their yard, so you'll need to find another spot (like your *other* neighbor's yard).

6. Next, frame the walls and floor with rebar and wood.

7. You'll probably want to fill your pool with water at some point, so now you'll need to play plumber. Dig a trench and run a pipe from your house connection to the pool.

8. Install the filtration system. Once that's in place, get ready to dust off your electrical skills. Dig another trench and run a power line to your pool. Install the pool lights next and cover up those trenches.

9. Mix the concrete and pour the floor. Then grade and smooth it. Once the cement is dry, line the walls with cinder blocks. Fill any space between the blocks and the soil around the pool with appropriate filling material: clay in an arid climate, or gravel in a wetter place.

10. Prepare the mortar and line the cinder block walls with the tiles. Once everything's dried, turn on the water and wait for the pool to fill. Then turn on the lights. Before you dip your toes in the water, you'll want to make sure that you ran that power line correctly. Toss the turkey in the pool. If it gets fried, that means you messed something up. If so, kill the power and figure out where you went wrong.

11. If the turkey sinks to the bottom without incident, that's a good sign that you won't electrocute yourself when you dive in to retrieve it (do this now).

12. Next, add the chlorine. This will help keep the water free from bacteria and algae. Be sure to use the correct amount for the size and depth of your pool. Tossing in too much could irritate your eyes and give you a nasty skin rash.

13. Finally, add the water slide, pool noodles, and that diving board if you've got 'em. Change into your swimsuit (or go *au naturel*) and get ready to become the envy of the entire neighborhood.

HOW TO MAKE SCRATCH-AND-SNIFF STICKERS

Scratch-and-sniff from scratch is definitely something to sniff at.

WHAT YOU'LL NEED

- Powdered adhesive. Look for it at a craft store—it's called "embossing powder." It's used to make paper items stand out from the page and provide three-dimensional heft.

- Lemon-scented essential oil

- Handheld heat gun (you can also get this at the craft store)

- Paintbrush

- Paper

- Paint

OR...WHAT YOU'LL NEED

- Unflavored gelatin (see page 84 to make your own)

- Water

- Electric mixer

- Lemon-scented essential oil

- Paintbrush

- Paper

- Paint

DO IT YOURSELF!

1. Mix the embossing powder in a shallow bowl with a fair amount of the essential oil.

2. Prepare the surface that you wish to make scratch-and-sniff-able. To make this easier for you, we've prepared this old-school scratch-and-sniff-esque image of a lemon making a kissy face. (It says "pucker up," because it's a lemon—get it?) Paint the picture yellow so it looks like a lemon.

3. While the ink is still wet on the picture, slather on with a paintbrush the goopy mixture of embossing powder and essential oil.

4. Blast the image with the heat gun. This will make the powder melt into a coating of microcapsules.

5. Let dry. Then scratch...and sniff.

OR...DO IT YOURSELF!

1. *Microencapsulation* occurs naturally in gelatin. Dissolve some in roughly half of the boiling water you'd use if you were going to cook it.

WHAT'S THAT SMELL?

The activation of scratch-and-sniff surfaces—
and their longevity—is due to the phenomenon of
microencapsulation. Clusters of thousands of microscopic
beads are glued to the surface, and each is a capsule
containing a tiny droplet of fragrance. Scratching the
sticker with a fingernail ruptures some of those capsules,
releasing scent particles. Only a few of those fragrance
drops are released each time, which means that a scratch-
and-sniff sticker can last for years.

2. Add in the scented oil, mixing thoroughly in
an electric mixer set on high.

3. When the mixture is cooled slightly but
before it starts to set, use the paintbrush to
apply a thin, even coat to our awesome, just-
colored lemon picture.

4. Let dry thoroughly. Then scratch...and sniff.

HOW TO MAKE SOAP

Saponification: *It's as easy as lye!*

WHAT YOU'LL NEED

- Several pounds of wood ash
- Barrel with the bottom cut out
- Stone slab to place the barrel onto, with a groove and lip carved into it
- Pile of rocks
- Water
- Straw and small sticks
- Wide clay bowl
- Several pounds of animal fat or used cooking grease
- Two large kettles
- Potato
- Salt (optional)

DO IT YOURSELF!

1. Soap is made by boiling together a potassium-based alkali extract called potash, obtained from wood ashes, and purified fat. To get the potash, you need to set up your potash-extraction station. Place the pile of

rocks on the ground (you'll want to do this outside—it's going to smell very bad), and on top of that, place the stone slab. Place the bottomless barrel atop the stone. Put the clay collection bowl below the barrel but in front of the rocks, so anything that comes out of the barrel will, eventually, wind up in it.

2. Line the bottom of the barrel with straw, grass, and sticks—this will prevent large chunks of ash from getting through.

3. Throw your wood ashes (any fireplace or campfire wood ash will do) into the barrel, on top of the straw.

4. Slowly pour warm water over the ashes. Continue until a brown liquid emerges into the clay bowl at the bottom. This is potash.

5. Set it aside.

6. The potash is ready, so now you need the other major ingredient: clean fat. Cut off any visible meat chunks that still remain on the

fat, if you're using tallow (beef fat) or lard (pig fat). You can also use accumulated cooking grease, but it will be rancid if it hasn't been refrigerated. This grease needs to be cleaned of impurities, too—cleaner fat or grease will make for a sweeter-smelling soap.

7. Get an outdoor fire going. Place the fat into a large kettle and add in an equal amount of water. Put the kettle over the open fire and boil it until all the fat has melted.

8. Boil it a little longer to make sure all the fat, even the fat you can't see, has completely melted.

9. Put out the fire, and pour into the kettle the same amount of water you poured into it at the beginning of the rendering process. Leave the fat/water mixture overnight to cool.

10. The next morning, you'll find that the fats have solidified and floated to the top of the kettle to form a layer of clean, thick, hardened fat. All the impurities have sunk into the water underneath the fat.

11. Throw out the water. Take the fat and transfer it to the other kettle. Combine it with the potash. How do you know if you've got the right amount? Place a raw potato into the solution. If it floats, leaving above the surface an area roughly akin to that of a quarter, it's good lye. If the potato sinks, it's too strong, so add water and stir. If the potato floats too much, the solution is weak and needs to be boiled down.

12. Place the kettle of potash and fat on the fire again and boil for six to eight hours, until the soap forms into a thick, frothy mass.

13. Taste the soap. Does it sting your tongue? Then keep boiling. It's ready when it lacks bite. If so, let it cool until it's a brown, jellylike liquid.

14. If you prefer bar-type soap, throw in a scoop of salt at the end of the boiling, right before cooling. A hard cake of soap will form on top.

HOW TO MAKE (A) FILM

Sure, you could shoot on digital, but doesn't your idea deserve richness and texture that only film can provide?

WHAT YOU'LL NEED

- An idea!
- Sets, costumes, actors, etc.
- Animal skin
- Silver
- Cotton or wood fibers
- Potassium nitrate (or acetic anhydride)
- Nitric acid
- Sulfuric acid
- Protective gloves
- Potassium bromide
- Metal or plastic trays
- Camera

SILVER STREAK

Thousands of early films have been lost forever. Why? The silver used to make the film stock was considered more valuable than the films, so the master copies were melted down to recover the silver.

DO IT YOURSELF!

1. Grind the cotton or wood fibers into cellulose, then mix it with potassium nitrate or acetic anhydride until it forms a clear, thick liquid. BE CAREFUL! Cellulose nitrate is extremely combustible; it caused many cinema fires and deaths in the early 20th century.

2. Without blowing yourself up, cast the liquid into a smooth, even layer to dry. Now you've got your film base.

3. Soak the animal skin in a solution made up of the nitric and sulfuric acids. Boil it until the gelatin is released. Skim the gelatin off and store it in your fridge. You'll use this later.

4. You will need to get your hands on some silver. Try digging in an area known to have silver deposits, such as Mexico. Alternatively, you could open a kiosk at the mall and buy silver coins and jewelry from very desperate people at bargain-basement prices.

5. Whether your silver comes from ore you have mined or Grandma's old brooch, you will need to melt it down and isolate the pure silver through either smelting or chemical leaching.

6. Dissolve the pure silver with nitric acid to form silver nitrate. Wear gloves because nitric acid reacts with fats and proteins to decompose living tissue.

7. As it cools, the silver nitrate will form into crystals. These crystals are the light-sensitive material that will capture the images of your dreams. Also, because of that light sensitivity, the upcoming work with dangerous chemicals and industrial equipment must be done completely in the dark.

8. Remember the gelatin you made earlier? Grind the gelatin and combine it with the silver nitrate crystals and potassium bromide, forming a liquid emulsion.

9. Pour the liquid emulsion over the highly explosive film base you made earlier. Let the

emulsion dry, then cut your newly made film stock into strips you can feed through your film camera.

10. Hire actors and a crew, shoot, and edit your story.

FIRE IN THE HOLE

Nitrate film base was essentially the same material as gun cotton, an explosive propellant once used in mines, torpedoes, and fictional moonshots (see page 165). The material is very sensitive: the heat from a film projector could cause the film inside to ignite. Once nitrate film stock started burning, nothing could put it out, not sand, foam, or submersion in water, because it supplied its own oxygen. As cinema fires became common, some cities mandated that projection booths be constructed as fireproof boxes of concrete and steel. This could protect the patrons in the theater, although the poor projectionist was likely to go down with his ship.

HOW TO BUILD MOUNT RUSHMORE

Think the heads on Mount Rushmore are a natural rock formation? Think again! It wasn't erosion that carved those presidential portraits into the Black Hills of South Dakota—it was good ol' American know-how, a ton of cash...and a lot of explosives.

WHAT YOU'LL NEED

- A suitable mountainside capable of supporting several 60-foot-tall heads
- About 400 laborers
- Temporary housing
- $989,992.32 in 1941 dollars (about $128 million today)
- Dynamite
- Drills, chisels, and other rock-carving equipment
- Hand facer
- Silicon sealant
- More dynamite
- Plaster

DO IT YOURSELF!

1. Select four great American presidents. Be very sure of your selections unless you have a surplus of mountains.

2. Craft a scale model from plaster to give you some idea what the finished project will look like; trust us, you don't want your architect "eyeballing" it with live explosives.

3. Prepare the site. Erect temporary living quarters for your hundreds of workers. Don't forget the time clock! The workers who sculpted Rushmore climbed 700 stairs every morning to punch in.

4. Ninety percent of your carving will be done with dynamite. Lower your drillers onto the rock face with cables. Make blast holes with jackhammers. Your powdermen will load these with carefully measured amounts of TNT, calculated to remove precise quantities of mountainside.

5. Get everyone clear, and boom goes the dynamite!

MONUMENTS MEN

South Dakota state historian Doane Robinson conceived the idea of transforming the Black Hills mountain range into a monument to America's greatest presidents. The design was sculpted by Danish-American Gutzon Borglum, who oversaw the project from 1927 until his death in 1941. His son, Lincoln, supervised the final months of construction.

6. Repeat with thousands of individual explosions, until the shape of the monument is roughed out.

STILL WAITING

Mount Rushmore isn't technically finished. The original plan called for the presidents to be depicted in head and chest, like four monumental busts.

7. When the rock is within six inches or so of the final carving surface, it's time to switch to hand tools. Drill shallow holes very close together—a technique called "honeycombing"—until the rock can be removed with chisels.

8. Smooth up the finished product with a hand facer, and seal it with silicon.

9. Once completed, sell tickets to see your monument at $85 per person.

HOW TO MAKE CONCRETE

Our instructions? They're pretty solid. As solid as, well, uh, concrete.

WHAT YOU'LL NEED

- A rock quarry
- Limestone
- Chalk
- Shale clay
- Dynamite
- Rock mill
- Paper ash
- Industrial kiln
- Rock-crushing equipment, like a sledgehammer
- Conveyor belt
- Gypsum
- Water
- Cement mixer
- Industrial oven

HARD ROCK

• Concrete is a mixture of portland cement, coarse aggregate (different types of stones), fine aggregate (different grades of sand), chemical admixtures, and water.

• Cement and concrete are not the same thing. Cement is the powdered substance that water is mixed with to create concrete, crystallizing in the mixture.

DO IT YOURSELF!

1. Gain access to a quarry rich with various naturally occurring mineral rocks, particularly limestone, chalk, shale, or clay.

2. Using a lot of dynamite, blast these rocks to smithereens.

3. From the limestone, chalk, shale, or clay, extract calcium carbonate, silica, alumina, and iron ore.

SOFT ROCK

Additions may be included to give concrete properties such as reduced permeability, greater resistance to sulfates, improved workability, or higher finish.

4. Crush the minerals.

5. Add in paper ash, which will ensure smoother cement.

6. Mill them to produce a fine powder known as raw meal.

7. Preheat it in an industrial oven to about 500°F.

8. Send the raw meal to a conveyor-driven kiln. Heat it to around 3,600°F (a temperature similar to that of molten lava). It's so hot that the very chemical structure of all those rocks change. The concrete industry's name for this is "cement clinker."

9. Angle the kiln by 3 degrees horizontally. This allows material to pass through the kiln.

10. Let your rocks take about 20 to 30 minutes to cool.

11. Cool the clinker.

12. Add in about 3 to 5 percent gypsum to the clinker. This will make the cement ultimately set better.

13. Grind everything once more.

14. Mix with water inside a cement mixer.

15. Pour out the cement into a hole.

16. Smooth it out, and play jacks on your new sidewalk.

HOW TO CREMATE A BODY

Here's another way to shuffle off the mortal coil of someone else that doesn't involve as many chemicals (see page 68): setting it on fire.

WHAT YOU'LL NEED

- A body
- Several dozen wooden logs or slats of uniform size
- Metal frame
- Kindling, newspaper, fire-starting log
- An accelerant, such as lighter fluid or kerosene
- Matches
- Five one-gallon buckets

SOMETHING'S COOKIN'

• The modern process of cremation uses industrial ovens that can reach temperatures north of 2,000°F.

• During cremation, it's common for the deceased to move his arms, or even sit up. As the muscle tissue burns, it contracts (similar to how a slice of cooking bacon will curl at the edges). While sitting forward is uncommon, it's likely his arms will contract into what funeral directors call the "pugilistic pose," as if he were a boxer raising his fists to defend his face.

DO IT YOURSELF!

1. A regular oven isn't hot enough or large enough to reduce a nonliving human body to ash. But you can still do it yourself with a homemade funeral pyre. On first glance, a pyre may look like just a pile of wood, but it must be constructed in a specific way to generate the heat necessary to turn your loved one into ash. Basically, you will be building a Jenga tower, so it's important that your slats are uniform or your pyre will be lopsided, and Uncle Jerry may topple off midway through the burn. Start by placing a metal frame or grate from which to build the pyre. This will get the wood up off the ground and allow airflow underneath.

2. Stack your wood in layers, with each layer crisscrossing the layer below for stability. You should also make each layer a little smaller than the one below, so that your pyre narrows as the stacks grow higher. This narrowing will create a chimney effect during the burn, concentrating the heat near the top and allowing you to reach a maximum temperature of around 800°F. That's no industrial cremator, but it will get the job done.

3. Lay your loved one atop the pyre and light 'er up. Try to start the fire as near to the center as possible, to encourage an even burn. (Again, it helps to have a metal frame that allows you to reach underneath the pyre.)

4. You can speed along the burn with an accelerant like kerosene, but keep in mind that if your loved one was an "all-natural" type, this may be against his or her wishes.

5. It will take around five hours for the body to be completely cremated. Whereas in modern cremation, the ashes (mostly bone) are collected for the family, the remnants from a corpse burned over a pyre will be mostly indistinguishable from the ashes from the burned wood. So if you do want to collect and spread the ashes somewhere, plan to bring about five one-gallon buckets.

HOW TO MAKE DORITOS

"Doritos" is Spanish for "little pieces of gold," and Doritos have certainly been a gold mine for their maker, Frito-Lay, which does $13 billion in business annually. However, they're as much the result of complicated chemistry as actual gold.

WHAT YOU'LL NEED

- Whole corn
- Food-grade lye
- Strainer
- Triangle press
- Deep-fryer
- Corn, sunflower, and soybean oils
- Salt
- Dextrose (a sugar)
- Corn maltodextrin (a sugar)
- Powdered milk
- Various cheese and dairy cultures (see below)
- Spices (see below)
- Chemical flavors and additives (see below)

CHIP, CHIP, HOORAY

Doritos were invented by Arch West, V.P. of Marketing at Frito-Lay, after seeing people eat fried tortilla chips while on a family vacation. When West passed away in 2011, his family sprinkled Doritos crumbs over his grave instead of dirt.

DO IT YOURSELF!

1. Heat the corn and soak in a solution of water and food-grade lye. This will denature the corn and break it down into a mush. Place the corn mush in a strainer and gently rinse off all the lye.

2. Roll the corn mush into tiny balls. With a triangle-shaped press, flatten and form the corn balls into little triangles.

3. Heat up a deep-fryer full of a mixture of corn, sunflower, and soybean oils. Don't skimp on the oil—the corn base will suck the stuff right up. (Store-bought Doritos are about 30 percent fat by weight.)

4. When they're brown and crispy, remove the corn chips from the oil and let them stand on paper towels. Do not fully air dry or pat them down. The oil will help the many, many, many flavorings stick to the chips.

5. Mix together a base of salt, dextrose, corn maltodextrin, and powdered milk. Fun fact:

The one-two-three punch of fat, salt, and sugar triggers the release of natural opioids in the human brain, which is why snack foods like this are so addictive and nearly impossible to eat in small quantities.

BET YOU CAN'T EAT JUST ONE

In his book *Why Humans Like Junk Food,* food scientist Steve Witherly figured out why Doritos are so addictive. It's because they've been chemically designed to be that way. The garlic flavor creates "long hang-time flavors" that leave behind a smell and "food memories" that your brain finds pleasant. Further, not one of the many flavors in Doritos overpowers another, so none linger. If one did, your brain would register "sensory specific satiety," or fullness. Lactic acid and citric acid are included, which makes saliva flow, stimulating appetite.

6. Now it's time to sprinkle, coat, and toss the chips with specific flavorings. What you use depends on which unique flavor of Doritos you're trying to mimic.

- For **Nacho Cheese**, you'll need dehydrated tomato powder, paprika, powdered cheddar cheese cultures, and chili powder.

- For **Cool Ranch**, you'll want powdered buttermilk and sour cream cultures, onion powder, garlic powder, and freeze-dried herbs: chives, dill, and parsley, all ground into powders.

- The **All-Nighter Cheeseburger** flavor calls for cheddar and Swiss cheese cultures, onion powder, ground mustard seed, and down-home favorites like 4-hydroxy-5-methyl-3(2H)-furanone, 2-methyl-3-furanthiol, and bis(2-methyl-3-furyl) disulfide.

JUST LIKE HOMEMADE

The ingredients 4-hydroxy-5-methyl-3(2H)-furanone, 2-methyl-3-furanthiol, and bis(2-methyl-3-furyl) disulfide are chemical by-products left from distilling the water out of clarified beef broth, so they're technically "natural flavorings," like it says on a bag of Doritos.

HOW TO CONSTRUCT A SOLAR PANEL

The sun. Giving off all that energy, and so much of it going to waste. Put that sun to work, once and for all!

WHAT YOU'LL NEED

- Quartz sand
- Rock-crushing equipment
- Electric arc furnace
- Cylindrical mold
- Graphite-lined crucible
- Boron-tempered silicon crystal
- Cylindrical furnace
- Heat-resistant cable
- Saw with diamond blade
- Wire saw
- Liquid abrasive
- Metal rack
- Lattice wire
- Clean room
- Texture etch
- High-temperature oven
- Phosphorus gas
- Blue-purple nitride
- Copper electrical circuitry
- Copper wire
- Metal connectors
- Steel frame
- Precision knife
- Liquid glass
- Junction box with conduit
- Solar cell battery

DO IT YOURSELF!

1. To build a solar panel, you must craft one out of photovoltaic solar cells, essentially thin slices of extremely pure silicon that convert sunlight into electricity. So first you'll need silicon. Find a quartz sand quarry and get to mining. If you don't get any from the quarry, dredge sand and gravel from a beach, an inland sand dune, or a riverbed.

2. Crush the accumulated rocks until it all has the consistency of sand.

3. Sort out the silica from the dirt, refuse, and other minerals. This isn't pure silicon yet— it's silicon dioxide, or one molecule of silicon fused to two molecules of oxygen. Bounded to oxygen is how silicon is found in its natural state, and it has to be purified.

SUNSHINE STATE

The state with the largest solar power capacity per capita is Arizona. That's due in part to year-round sunshine, as well as large tax incentives for solar power creators and adopters.

4. Place the silicon dioxide into an electric arc furnace. There, a carbon arc and a temperature of 5,800°F will release the oxygen from the silicon. This will result in two substances: waste carbon dioxide and molten silicon. Get rid of the carbon dioxide.

5. Heat the silicon until it's white-hot and pour it into a long, cylindrical mold. There, the molten silicon will re-fuse into crystals, with all of its atoms aligning into the proper orientation.

6. Take the silicon rocks and stack them inside the graphite-lined crucible along with a silicon disk treated with boron. That one will serve as a seed crystal, and also ensure proper electrical functioning later.

7. Place the crucible inside the cylindrical furnace. Heat it to 2,500°F.

8. The silicon will melt into a soupy, slushy slurry. As it does, extend the boron-treated seed crystal via a cable into the hot liquid.

9. As the crystal hardens, slowly retract the seed crystal.

10. Let the silicon cool to 300°F. It should take about two and a half days.

11. Open the crucible and remove the cylindrical silicon crystal.

12. Now the silicon has to be cut into a wafer shape to make the photovoltaic cells.

13. Using a saw with a diamond blade, cut off the top and bottom off the crystal to create a uniform cylinder of silicon. Draw the wire-blade saw treated with liquid abrasive across the surface to cut the crystal into ingots. Mount one end into a steel rack and use lattice wire to cut the silicon into squares.

14. Cut the ingots into very thin wafers, about 0.3 mm thick.

15. Take the wafers into your clean room. With a texture etch, remove the top layer of the silicon wafer, revealing an irregular pyramid pattern that is more light-absorbent than a smooth surface.

16. Place the wafers in a high-temperature oven set at 1,500°F, and apply a thin layer of phosphorus gas. This will electrically charge the wafers.

17. Apply the blue-purple nitride to the top layer of the wafer. This reduces reflection (you want them to absorb light, after all).

18. Apply metal circuitry and soldered cells together into strings of 10. Connect six strings of 10 wafers to create a panel of 60

cells. Mount into a metal frame and laminate with glass.

19. Connect the panel to a junction box with a conduit, and then to a solar cell.

20. Collect all that sweet, sweet sunlight, and feel free to leave all your lights and appliances on for the rest of eternity.

HOW TO MAKE PLASTIC

"Plastic" is an umbrella term for a range of solid materials composed of long-chain molecules called polymers. Industrial plastics are made from petroleum, and require access to exotic and incredibly toxic chemicals. But using the same chemical principles, you can make your own organic plastic at home from common kitchen items.

WHAT YOU'LL NEED

- Heavy-bottomed saucepan
- 1 cup whole milk (the higher the fat content, the better; heavy cream is even better)
- 5–6 tablespoons white vinegar
- Fine-mesh strainer
- Formaldehyde

DON'T BE CRUDE

The polymers that make up plastics are themselves formed out of shorter molecular chains called monomers, which are mostly composed of carbon atoms. In oil-based plastic, the process is the same as with our milk plastic; a chemical catalyst is added to crude oil, causing the monomers to clump and link together on a molecular level. The resulting clusters of polymers are then heated to fuse them into plastic solids.

DO IT YOURSELF!

1. In the saucepan, heat the milk or cream to a simmer, being careful not to boil.

2. Add your vinegar a tablespoon at a time, stirring gently as you do. The milk will curdle, forming solid clumps. The vinegar is forcing a chemical reaction, causing a protein called casein to precipitate out of the milk.

   YOU CAN DO IT!

   The first mass-marketed plastic items from the dawn of the 20th century were clothing buttons made using this exact process.

3. Pour the whole mess through a strainer, then squeeze out the remaining moisture.

4. You now have a soft, rubbery solid that can be sculpted or molded. Your casein "plastic" won't have much of a shelf life by itself; it will spoil in a few days if untreated.

5. After you have molded the casein plastic into the desired shape, immerse in formaldehyde and let dry to cure and harden it permanently.

HOW TO MAKE ALKALINE BATTERIES

And you were probably just going to throw away all that manganese dioxide left over from your last party, weren't you? Use it to make AA or AAA batteries instead.

WHAT YOU'LL NEED

- Tiny hollow steel drum the size of the battery you'll need
- Powdered zinc
- Powdered manganese dioxide
- Electrolytic solution of liquid potassium hydroxide
- Coal dust
- Brass "collector pin"
- Plastic-cover seal cap
- External lead end cap, positive (+)
- External lead end cap, negative (−)
- Porous synthetic plate separator—in other words, some special thick paper

DO IT YOURSELF!

1. Soak the porous synthetic plate separator paper in the liquid potassium hydroxide. Set aside.

2. Take the hollow steel drum, which serves as the battery's casing, houses all the working parts, and assists the performance of the cathode. Mix the powdered manganese dioxide with the coal dust inside the steel drum.

POWER UP

• To create an electrochemical reaction inside a battery, there must be two electrodes. One is positively charged, called an anode, and the other is negatively charged, called a cathode. Inside the battery, the anode and cathode are surrounded by a solution called an electrolyte. That solution can be in liquid, paste, or powder form.

• A chemical reaction causes electrons to build up in the anode. When the battery is connected to an electronic device like a flashlight and the device is turned on, the electrons flow from the anode, through the device, to the cathode.

3. Heat the drum, melting the manganese-coal solution. Let it adhere to the inner wall of the steel drum. The cathode is now complete.

4. Fit the electrolyte-treated paper on top of the cathode-lined casing.

5. Fill the remaining space inside the battery (and within the porous plate separator paper) with zinc powder and more of the potassium hydroxide.

6. Insert the brass pin in the middle of the battery, from the bottom. This collector pin collects the negative charge.

7. The brass pin is in touch with the lead end cap—just inside that, place the plastic cover. That separates the steel drum from the caps, which have different charges. Seal the end with its lead cap: (+) on the top, (–) on the bottom.

8. Insert the battery in your electronic device.

9. Go to a hospital to get treated for chemical burns and mild electrical shock.

HOW TO BUILD A SPORTS CAR FROM SCRATCH

A super-fast fancy car like the ones you had on posters in your bedroom when you were 14 will run you more than $100,000, and that's not even including the options package.

WHAT YOU'LL NEED

- Approximately 40 sheets of fiberglass
- Plenty of tubular steel
- A high-performance engine
- 1 gallon of primer
- 3 gallons of auto paint
- Welding torch
- Protective gear
- Motor oil, transmission fluid, and other auto fluids
- Lots and lots of car parts (see below)
- Car design software and a computer to run it on
- Blueprints

DO IT YOURSELF!

1. Design a blueprint for your car so you have at least a vague idea of what the final product should look like. Feel free to add cool fins and a racing stripe or two.

2. Head to the garage and get ready to build the framework (a.k.a., the chassis) for your car out of the tubular steel. If you've never used a welding torch, stop what you're doing and enroll in a welding class. While you're at it, sign up for a few courses in auto tech if you slept through shop class in high school. When all that's out of the way, weld all the tubes together until they're in the shape of a car.

3. Once you've managed to build the chassis, it's time to get started on the engine. We suggest buying the necessary parts online or elsewhere, but if you want to complete this project truly "from scratch," prepare yourself for a labor-intensive process that could require hundreds of hours. Constructing a carburetor out of raw materials isn't easy, you know.

4. You'll also need a steering wheel, seats, a dashboard, an odometer, a fuel gauge, an exhaust pipe, a clutch, upholstery, wheels, tires, a few pedals, shocks, a gas tank, a vinyl or hardtop roof, windows, a starter, a key, and door handles, in addition to speakers and a radio if you enjoy listening to something other than various pieces of your homemade car falling off and hitting the pavement while you drive it. You could technically build all these things from scratch, but salvaging parts from a junkyard might be a better idea.

5. Next, you'll need to make the molds required for the various components that comprise the car's body (i.e., the hood, the doors, etc.). First, you'll need to design some plugs, which are the frameworks you'll use to make each mold. For example, to make a fender, you'll need a plug shaped like a fender. Some people use clay or wood, but Styrofoam often works best.

6. Once you've worked the plugs into the shape of each component, grab some of those fiberglass sheets. Put a sheet over each plug

and cover them in a polyester or ISO resin. Make sure there aren't any air pockets or fibers visible. Let the resin on each mold harden a bit, but apply the second round of sheets while it's still tacky. Repeat this process a few more times. You may need three or four sheets for each mold.

CAR, JACK

In 2008, Oregon automobile enthusiast Jack McCornack salvaged engine parts from an old Toyota Corolla, and then took some from a beat-up Kubota tractor. Along with another $10,000 worth of materials, he built a street-legal sports car. Unlike other sports cars, it's gas-efficient, with McCornack reporting an impressive 100 miles per gallon.

7. It'll take two or three days for each mold to "cure" before it's ready to be removed from its plugs. Once that's done, sand and polish each one.

8. Connect the molds to the chassis and get ready to do some painting. The primer comes first. Apply the first coat, wait for it to cure,

then apply the second coat. You may need a third coat before it's time to use the actual automotive paint. Repeat the process with the paint. You'll need three to four layers before you finally give the molds a good shine with a buffer.

9. Drop the engine into the car and install the other components. Don't forget the steering wheel! You'll definitely need that for the final step.

10. Dump in all the necessary fluids and pour some gas in the tank.

11. Jump into the driver's seat and turn the key. With any luck, your new sports car will actually make it to the end of the street.

HOW TO MAKE COCA-COLA

Who doesn't enjoy an ice-cold Coca-Cola on a hot summer day? But buying yourself one from the store can cost into the tens of cents.

WHAT YOU'LL NEED

- Cane sugar or high-fructose corn syrup (see page 29)
- Caramel color
- Phosphoric acid
- Coca extract
- Lime extract
- Vanilla
- Orange oil
- Lemon oil
- Nutmeg oil
- Caffeine
- Citric acid
- Cinnamon
- Nutmeg
- Coriander

- Neroli (bitter orange tree oil)
- "Coca extract" in liquid form (otherwise known as cocaine)
- Carbonated water
- Stockpot

COKE IS IT!

While there was "coca" in Coca-Cola, there was never any "cola," or extract of the kola nut. The cinnamon and vanilla combination imitates the natural (and more expensive) kola fairly well.

DO IT YOURSELF!

1. Mix the cane sugar (or HFCS), caramel color, phosphoric acid, lime extract, orange oil, lemon oil, nutmeg oil, and vanilla together in a stockpot. Simmer over low heat for about an hour until it reduces into a syrup, or the basis of the drink.

2. The actual blend of spices in Coca-Cola is a tightly held trade secret, which purportedly is known by only a select few employees. Based on the results of a few re-creations attempted over the years by various journalists and food scientists, use the remaining spices, oils, and extracts listed above. Or, start with cinnamon and nutmeg, which are confirmed to be a part of Coke, and go from there, experimenting with adding other spices to your syrup until you feel like you've hit the sweet spot.

3. The original 19th-century Coca-Cola recipe promised to provide pep to whoever consumed it, and they weren't kidding—it famously included cocaine. ("Coca" *is* right there in the name.) John Pemberton's original recipe called for coca leaf extract, an estimated 9 mg of cocaine per serving. Coca leaf is quite illegal in the U.S., as is cocaine, so unless you're willing to put your freedom on the line, skip this step and just use caffeine.

4. Once your syrup has chilled, mix it with carbonated water (or club soda), and voilà! You've got Coca-Cola. Commercially produced Coke is 86% water, so you'll want to shoot for a similar ratio in your batch of not-quite "The Real Thing."

THE SECRET'S SAFE

• The good news is, you don't have to be a an ex-Confederate soldier hooked on morphine to make Coca-Cola, although inventor John Pemberton was. Today, it's made from mostly water, corn syrup, and a flavor profile called "7X," the exact recipe of which is kept sealed in an Atlanta bank vault.

• One 20-ounce bottle of Coke contains 15 teaspoons of sweetener.

• In 2011, producers of *This American Life* re-created Coca-Cola based on a blurry 1979 newspaper photo of the original recipe in an article about Pemberton. Taste-testers said the resulting Coke was close…but not perfect.

HOW TO MAKE PAPER

A piece of commercially produced paper costs a fraction of a cent. Or you could make your own at a much higher cost and with many hours of arduous labor.

WHAT YOU'LL NEED

- A hardwood tree, such as oak or maple
- A softwood tree, like pine or spruce
- Axe or chainsaw
- Peeling iron
- Pressure washer
- Wood grinder
- Wood chipper
- Tubs of water
- Bleach
- A meshed screen, called a wire
- Felt rollers
- Metal silo

- Hot steam shooters
- Hot rollers
- Calender (iron press)
- Fine clay
- Spools
- Paper slicer

HIGH IN FIBER

Wood is made up of tiny strands of cellulose that stick together because of a natural adhesive called lignin. The splitting and restructuring of those fibers is how paper is made.

DO IT YOURSELF!

1. With the axe or chainsaw, chop down your hardwood tree. Then, chop down your softwood tree. Remove branches, too.

2. Remove the bark with a peeling iron to expose the inner wood of both trees.

3. Wash off all remaining dirt, sap, and debris with a high-powered pressure washer. Allow the wood to dry.

4. Slowly feed each log through a wood chipper.

5. Pour the combined wood chips into a water bath, which will separate out the wood fibers from the wood parts you won't need. Take the fibers and place them in another bath consisting of bleach and water. The resulting pulp will be 99 percent watery mush, but these are the wood fibers you'll use to make paper.

6. Place the pulp on a long, thin meshed screen called a wire. Much of the water will drain

out, leaving the fibers to collect and bind together into something called a "fiber mat."

7. Squeeze the fiber mat through felt rollers. This will press out more water, but the wood pulp is still a mushy mess of approximately two-thirds water.

8. Place the paper pulp into a metal silo filled with hot steam and also outfitted with more hot rollers. Run the pulp through the rollers while the hot steam shoots at it. The heating and drying moves the fibers closer together, gradually forming lumpy rolls of almost-paper.

9. Run the rolls through the calender, in which iron rollers press the paper into uniform thickness (or thinness).

10. Coat the paper in a fine layer of fine clay. This will make the writing surface smoother and more uniform. Let it dry.

11. Roll the paper onto spools. Cut into sheets.

HOW TO MAKE TWINKIES

*Twinkies have a shelf life of around two months,
and it's all thanks to just a few dozen chemicals.*

WHAT YOU'LL NEED

- Aluminum foil
- Piping bags
- Spice bottle
- Bleached wheat flour
- Folic acid
- Niacin
- Thiamin
- Riboflavin
- Ferrous sulfate (iron)
- Sugar
- Water
- Corn syrup
- High fructose corn syrup
- Vegetable shortening
- Animal shortening
- Egg
- Dextrose
- Modified cornstarch
- Corn flour
- Glucose
- Baking soda
- Monocalcium phosphate
- Sodium acid pyrophosphate
- Sweet dairy whey
- Soy protein isolate
- Calcium caseinate
- Sodium caseinate
- Soy flour
- Salt
- Monoglycerides
- Diglycerides
- Polysorbate 60

- Corn dextrin
- Soy lecithin
- Cornstarch
- Cellulose gum
- Sodium steroyal lactylate
- Sorbic acid
- FD&C Yellow #5
- Red 40
- Calcium sulfate (food-grade version of plaster of Paris)

DO IT YOURSELF!

1. Wrap 12 pieces of aluminum foil around a Twinkie-sized object, like a spice bottle, to make 12 molds. Remove the bottle (unless you really enjoy cinnamon-and-plastic-filled Twinkies).

2. Preheat the oven to 350°F.

3. First, make the cake batter. Since this is baking, you've got to mix the dry ingredients together first. In a large bowl, combine the bleached wheat flour, folic acid, niacin, thiamin, riboflavin, ferrous sulfate, sugar, monoglyceride and diglyceride (they emulsify and mimic eggs, sorbic acid (a mold preventer), salt, modified cornstarch, corn flour, corn dextrin, soy flour, soy protein isolate, baking soda, sodium acid pyrophosphate (a shelf-stable baking powder replacement), dextrose, sweet dairy whey, FD&C Yellow #5, and Red

40 (those last two are food dyes which will combine to give the cake a nice yellow color).

4. Combine the wet ingredients: a single real egg (for leavening), the shortenings (to make the cakes last longer than they would with butter), water, and liquid glucose.

5. Make the cream filling, or, since it's non-dairy, "creme" filling. Whip together sugar, water, corn syrup, high fructose corn syrup, cellulose gum (a shelf-stable fat substitute and creaminess enhancer), polysorbate 60 (another shelf-stable fat substitute and creaminess enhancer), cornstarch, sodium caseinate (a milk protein), calcium sulfate (a coagulant), sodium steroyal lactylate (an emulsifier), soy lecithin (ditto), monocalcium phosphate, and calcium caseinate (another milk protein).

6. Pour batter into molds, bake for 10 minutes.

7. Let cool, and turn the molds over to release the cakes. Poke three holes into each cake with the tip of the piping bag, and fill each one with three dollops of creme filling.

HOW TO MAKE MARGARINE

Margarine: It's the plasticlike substance...you can eat!

WHAT YOU'LL NEED

- Oil press
- Cottonseed
- Rapeseed
- Hexane
- Several large bowls
- Steam cleaner
- Sieve
- Spoons
- Food steamer
- Powdered nickel
- Hydrogenation chamber
- Hydrogen gas
- Monoglycerides
- Food-grade bleach
- Yellow food dye

DO IT YOURSELF!

1. The first step is extracting oil from cottonseed and rapeseed. Light the wick on the oil press, fill the hopper with seeds, and allow 15 minutes for everything to heat up.

2. Once it's hot enough, hand-crank the press until the seeds give forth their precious oil.

3. Despite all that heat, pressure, and cranking, there is still some oil left in those seeds. As an industrial margarine maker would, collect your mostly spent seeds and soak them in hexane, an industrial solvent that's very effective at attracting plant-based oils.

4. Using a sieve and a bowl, carefully separate the seed husks from the oil, and from the hexane. Throw away the seed husks, and skim the oil off the top (that's the good thing about oil—it separates from other liquids). Try to get as little hexane as possible in your oil, because it's a carcinogen.

5. Collect the oil in a bowl, and place in your food steamer. Turn it on as high as it can go. While this step will kill off a lot of the nutrition in the oil, it will also destroy any remaining pesticides and hexane.

6. Once the oil has been steamed, mix into the bowl some powdered nickel—it will serve as a catalyst in "hydrogenation," the chemical process that turns the oil into a butterlike substance.

7. Place the treated oil into the hydrogenation chamber. Along with high temperatures, hydrogen gas will transform the oil molecules until the whole substance turns into a semisolid—or rather lumpy, gray grease.

8. Mix in the monoglycerides. These are industrially produced distilled vegetable fatty acids that serve as emulsifiers—in other words, they smooth out the lumps.

9. Return the mixture to the steam cleaner, in order to remove any remaining chemical odors.

10. Mix in food-grade bleach, which will turn the margarine to a slightly more appetizing white.

11. Add in the yellow food dye to make the margarine look like butter.

12. Form into sticks, or pour into plastic containers.

13. Ask your friends if they can't believe it's not butter. (If they can believe it's not butter...try again.)

HOW TO MAKE FOIE GRAS

*Examine the controversy yourself,
up close and personally.*

WHAT YOU'LL NEED

- Baby duck of the Mule or Muscovy variety
- Cage to keep the baby duck
- Larger cage to keep the duck after it starts growing
- 20 pounds of grain
- 50 pounds of corn
- 2 pounds of duck fat
- Manual screw dispenser, a tool that consists of a funnel, tube, and auger
- Stick
- Feedbag
- Feeding tube
- Butcher knife
- Paring knife
- Food scale
- Large bowl
- 1 liter of cold milk
- Paper towels
- Foil
- Salt and pepper
- Cognac
- Plastic wrap
- Glass pot with a sealable lid
- Terrine, or other small ceramic dish
- Baking dish

DO IT YOURSELF!

1. Check and make sure that what you're doing is legal. Force-feeding for the sake of foie gras production has been banned throughout the world, including in California, Argentina, Israel, and almost all of the European Union except for some regions of France where foie gras is of historical culinary importance.

2. Allow your baby duck to frolic, play, and grow for four weeks.

> **SACRE BLEU!**
>
> *Foie gras* is a French term that translates to "fatty liver." The finished food product is 85% fat.

3. At the end of the month, place your baby duck in a cage, and put the cage in a dark room. Feed it up to a pound of grain each day for four weeks.

4. When the duck is eight weeks old, move it to the larger cage, but continue to keep it shrouded in darkness.

5. For the next 21 days, subject the duck to *gavage*, or force-feeding. Place the end of the feeding tube down the duck's throat about five inches, *almost* to the point where the tube is in the duck's stomach, but not so far that it's choking.

6. Cook 1⅓ pounds of whole-grain corn in hot water until the kernels are soft. Add a small amount (2% of the total product) of duck fat, taken from ducks who have already been slaughtered. This does not make the duck's liver fattier—this fat is for lubricating the corn on its way down the feeding tube.

7. Pour the corn mixture into the funnel part of the manual screw dispenser. Turn the auger, forcing the corn through the funnel, down the tube, and into the duck's stomach. If the corn gets gummy and sticks in the tube, force it through with a stick.

8. Repeat this feeding procedure two more times that day. Continue to feed the duck this way three times a day for a total of 21 days. At the end of this three-week period, the duck's

liver will balloon from a weight of 80 grams to around 1,000 grams.

9. It's time to butcher the duck. The night before butchering, put it in a dark stall with water but don't feed it. This will clean out the digestive system and cut down on feces still in the duck.

10. Place the duck's head into an old feedbag. Cut a hole in the bag and poke the duck's head through. Gather the bag at the feet and hold it there, which prevents the animal from moving. Lay the bird down on a cutting surface and use the butcher knife to decapitate it in one quick motion.

11. Drain the blood.

12. Hose it down. Wash the feet and press down on the abdomen while rinsing to force out and wash away any feces.

13. Skinning the duck is easier than plucking its feathers. Starting at the neck, slip the paring knife under the skin where the head was.

Lift the skin and slice along the belly, moving down to the tail end. Pull the skin back and use the knife to separate the skin from the meat, working around the whole bird. Cut off the wings and legs.

14. Between the rib cage and the vent, make a shallow incision into the flesh on the belly side. Pull it open, pulling meat out of the way and away from the intestines. Cut around the vent to remove the internal organs.

15. Stuff your hand into the body cavity to pull out the gizzard, liver, and gallbladder all at once. The liver is the one that's gigantic.

16. Gently wash the liver. Leave it for 30 minutes in a pot of cold water.

17. Transfer it to the bowl and fill with a liter of cold milk, enough to submerge the liver. Add a tablespoon of salt, cover the bowl with foil, and refrigerate for 90 minutes. This will ease the removal of blood vessels while also tenderizing the meat.

18. Wipe the milk off the liver and put it on your work surface to remove the veins. First, separate the liver into its two lobes (this should happen naturally). Take the big lobe and find the Y-shaped veins. Following the natural grooves on the liver, press with your finger and make a little indentation along the way until you reach the vein's entry point. Insert your finger under the vein and pull gently until it detaches.

19. Do it again with the smaller lobe.

20. Sprinkle salt, pepper, and half a teaspoon of cognac onto the liver. Mold it back to its original form.

21. Place in the sealed glass pot and refrigerate for 12 hours.

22. Wipe the liver and place it in the small ceramic dish known as a terrine. Push and mold the liver to fit.

23. Place the terrine in the shallow baking dish

and fill with water heated to 160°F. Cover with a lid or foil.

24. Bake at 300°F for 40 minutes. The foie gras should reach an internal temperature of 150°F.

25. A lot of fat will cook off. Strain and keep only the yellow fat, and discard the liver juice.

26. Pour a thin layer of fat on the foie gras.

27. Cool to room temperature.

28. Cover, and then refrigerate for 24 hours.

29. Serve with toast points.

THE LAST PAGE

Fellow Bathroom Readers:

The fight for good bathroom reading should never be taken loosely—we must do our duty and sit firmly for what we believe in, even while the rest of the world is taking potshots at us.

We'll be brief. Now that we've proven we're not simply a flush-in-the-pan, we invite you to take the plunge:

Sit Down and Be Counted! Log on to *www.bathroomreader.com* and earn a permanent spot on the BRI honor roll!

If you like reading our books...VISIT THE BRI'S WEBSITE!
www.bathroomreader.com

- Receive our irregular newsletters via e-mail
- Order additional Bathroom Readers
- Face us on Facebook
- Tweet us on Twitter
- Blog us on our blog

Go with the Flow...

Well, we're out of space, and when you've gotta go, you've gotta go. Tanks for all your support. Hope to hear from you soon.

Meanwhile, remember...

KEEP ON FLUSHIN'!